# Forty Ways to Fortify Your Faith

## James R. Bjorge

**AUGSBURG** Publishing House • Minneapolis

*Dedicated to Mark and Jan Bjorge*

**Library of Congress Cataloging in Publication Data**

Bjorge, James R.
FORTY WAYS TO FORTIFY YOUR FAITH.

1. Christian life—Lutheran authors.   I. Title.
II. Title: 40 ways to fortify your faith.
BV4501.2.B536  1984        248.4'841        83-72115
ISBN 0-8066-2059-5 (pbk.)

Manufactured in the U.S.A.                                         APH 10-2358

2   3   4   5   6   7   8   9   0   1   2   3   4   5   6   7   8   9

# Contents

# Preface

When I was at the seminary the church was often described as the *church militant* and the *church triumphant*. The *church militant* meant the church on earth as it battles the forces of evil. The *church triumphant* was the assembly of faithful warriors who had fought "the good fight of faith" and had been transferred to the heavenly kingdom.

That terminology has largely been set on the shelf today. Some people in the pews even wince a bit when we sing hymns like "Onward, Christian Soldiers" or "Fight the Good Fight with All Your Might." We don't like war in any form, and words that conjure up conflict are taboo. There is so much trouble in the world that we want the church to be a tranquil sea where our little boats may dock safely and serenely.

All this is in sharp contrast to the early church. The recruiting of members was as though they were enlisting in the army. Paul tells Timothy, "Endure hardship with us like a good soldier of Christ Jesus. No one serving as a soldier gets involved in civilian affairs—he wants to please his commanding officer" (2 Tim. 2:3-4). To those early Christians the call of Christ was the summons of a commander to battle. They often had to forfeit business opportunities, cut themselves off from social attachments, struggle against the pull of old pagan associations.

Today we are tempted to call people into the church as a salesman offers a bargain. The stress is on what the church offers rather than what it requires. Prayer has sometimes been polluted as a way to get your share of goodies. Tithing is proclaimed as the door that leads to financial success.

Somewhere along the line we have given up the fight. And slowly and subtly the enemy has advanced. There has been an erosion of integrity. Our morals have been compromised. It is like a spiritual twilight zone where everything is vague.

We must recognize that a war is going on! Paul puts it like this: "For our struggle is not against flesh and blood, but against the rulers, against the authorities, against the powers of this dark world and against the spiritual forces of evil in the heavenly realms. Therefore put on the full armor of God, so that when the day of evil comes you may be able to stand your ground, and after you have done everything, to stand" (Eph. 6:12-13).

Realizing there is a raging battle, we have the opportunity to respond to Christ's challenge, not to safety but to service. While others offer a crown, he offers a cross. While others advise us to "eat, drink, and be merry," he says, "Deny yourself."

There was a resistance fighter in Norway in 1940 who was facing the invasion of his country. It looked hopeless for his native land. What should he do? Come to terms with the tyrants? Some were doing that. Or should he join the underground and risk his life? He made a decision and these were his words: "This is not a time for me to desert my faith. It is not a time to turn to new images of belief. This is a time for me to be dangerously faithful."

Is this kind of faithfulness too heavy for you and me? Would we rather watch the war than wage battle? I hope that this book will help awaken in us all the heroic aspects of the Christian faith. Then we shall salute our commander and follow him into the battle for righteousness in our time and place. The old hymn sums it up:

> They climbed the steep ascent of heav'n
> Thro' peril, toil, and pain:
> O God, to us may grace be given
> To follow in their train!

Finally, be strong in the Lord and in his mighty power.
Put on the full armor of God so that you can take your stand
against the devil's schemes.
For our struggle is not against flesh and blood,
but against the rulers, against the authorities,
against the powers of this dark world and against the spiritual
forces of evil in the heavenly realms.
Therefore, put on the full armor of God, so that when the day
of evil comes, you may be able to stand your ground,
and after you have done everything, to stand.
Stand firm then, with the belt of truth buckled around your waist,
with the breastplate of righteousness in place,
and with your feet fitted with the readiness that comes
from the gospel of peace.
In addition to all this, take up the shield of faith,
with which you can extinguish all the flaming arrows
of the evil one.
Take the helmet of salvation and the sword of the Spirit,
which is the word of God.
And pray in the Spirit on all occasions with all kinds of prayers
and requests. With this in mind, be alert
and always keep on praying for all the saints.
Pray also for me, that whenever I open my mouth,
words may be given me so that I will fearlessly make known
the mystery of the gospel, for which I am an ambassador in chains.
Pray that I may declare it fearlessly, as I should.

*Ephesians 6:10-20*

# 1

## The Power Connection

"Finally, be strong in the Lord and in his mighty power" (Eph. 6:10). Each of us needs an inner toughness, a measure of true grit. Neuroses are not to be coddled but challenged. Retreat is seldom the way to victory. Robert Frost once said, "The best way out is always through."

A noted warrior lived many centuries ago when men fought their battles with swords and shields. On the eve of a major conflict, this stouthearted man looked at his hands and saw that they trembled. His indomitable spirit reacted: "Tremble on; you would tremble more if you knew where I will take you today!" Such toughness is what most of us need for the road ahead.

Franklin Roosevelt was the American president who challenged the nation to defuse its fear as it floundered in the financial depression of the early 1930s. He told us that we had nothing to fear but fear itself. Yet he experienced considerable anxiety when all four of his sons were assigned to posts of danger during World War II. Eleanor Roosevelt is reported to have said to him, "You mustn't bring up your children like eagles and expect them to act like sparrows."

What is the church producing today? Eagles or sparrows? Eagles soar and ride the storm while sparrows cling to shelter. Faith finds its security in the flight and not taxiing up and down the runways at the airport. We were made for the stars and the splendor of the sky, but we so frequently have folded our wings and settled for a grubbing of worms in the soil.

How do we break out of the prison of timidity and live in a spirit of daring and toughness? The apostle Paul says that Christ is the power connection. He says, "Be strong in the Lord and in his mighty power." It means we are made powerful in Christ. The strengthening of our backbones is found in the vital energy which comes from union with Christ. Paul further explains, "I can do everything through him who gives me strength" (Phil. 4:13). In his letter to the Ephesians, Paul talks much about this power source. "Now to him who is able to do immeasurably more than all we ask or imagine, according to his power that is at work within us, to him be glory in the church and in Christ Jesus throughout all generations, for ever and ever! Amen" (3:20-21). And again, "His incomparably great power for us who believe . . . is like the working of his mighty strength which he exerted in Christ when he raised him from the dead and seated him at his right hand in the heavenly realms" (1:19-20).

Too often we look at our frailties and not at Christ's faculties. We measure his power by what we have seen in our own lives. Paul urges us to look around and get the full scope of the immeasurable greatness of God. A tide will lift a rowboat, but that certainly is not an indication of its power. A person who sees nothing beyond the end of his or her own dock will hardly be aware that the tide will lift the navies of the whole world and whatever else floats upon the oceans.

Power comes through an encounter with the limitless power of Jesus Christ. Antaeus was a mythical giant in old Greek legends. It was his custom to fight all who passed through his territory. He was always the winner. The opponents found to their dismay that no amount of beating Antaeus against the earth would subdue him. He would arise each time stronger and more refreshed than before. But Hercules guessed the secret of his strength. He realized Antaeus' strength and courage came from the earth, for he was the son of the goddess Earth. Therefore Hercules grasped the giant, kept him suspended in the air so he could not touch the earth, and squeezed him harder and harder until his life ebbed out of him.

In like manner, our strength comes from a vital union with Christ. He is our power connection. Live in him. There is our power for keeping on when the going is tough.

*Good strategy without good supply spells defeat.*

*2*

# Take It All

We are living in a supermarket society. The selections are many, so there is a system of pick-and-choose. A restaurant menu gives us many eating possibilities. Every major city has an abundance of television stations so we can flip from channel to channel in search of something to interest us.

Living in this environment we are susceptible to carrying it over into the arena of faith. We think we should have the right of choosing what we want in our religion. But Paul tells us, "Put on the full armor of God" (Eph. 6:13). Paul wants us to be complete, whole. He wants us to be prepared to fight the good fight of faith and come out as winners.

The ill-equipped soldier is vulnerable. So is the ill-equipped Christian. Choosing half the armor is leaving yourself open to the "flaming arrows of the evil one" (Eph. 6:16).

When you were a small child, as you left for school in the winter, your mother probably had many instructions: "Eat all your cereal because you need energy on this cold day. Put on your sweater, for the school room might be chilly. Wear your boots because it snowed three inches last night. Put on your mittens and cap and don't forget the scarf, because the wind is blowing like crazy this morning." You left for school bundled like a mummy, but you were warm and protected from the cold. Such is the love of a parent.

As a loving parent, God provides for us dress for the inevitable battle of life. We are to wear God's armor: the belt of truth, breastplate of righteousness, shoes of peace, shield of faith, and helmet of salvation.

Our problem today is not with the freedom of what to wear but with the faithfulness of wearing what he has given us. It is not adequate to say, "You follow Jesus in your way, and I will follow him in mine." As a child you wore what your mother dressed you in for the cold day. It was simply a matter of obedience. As children of God, or as enlisted men and women in the army of God, it is a matter of obedience too. We might call it commitment.

When Hitler attempted to control the church in Germany, some church leaders answered him in the Barmen Declaration of 1934. It boldly declared, "Jesus Christ . . . is the one Word of God, whom we have to trust and obey in life and death." When the armies of Caesar undertook the invasion of England they demonstrated an unusual commitment. As their little vessels appeared on the horizon, thousands of Englishmen gathered on the heights to defend their homeland. To their amazement, the first thing the Romans did upon disembarking was to set fire to their ships. As the flames destroyed their boats, there was no longer an avenue of escape. They were there to conquer, and with that type of commitment it is no wonder that they did!

The church needs to recover this daring obedience to the lordship of Christ. With no provision for retreating, we must fling ourselves upon the beaches of the world. If we wear the full armor that God gives, the victory will be ours. We may be fearful, but we will trust and obey, knowing a truth stated by Dietrich Bonhoeffer from a German prison, "I believe God will give us all the power we need. . . . But he never gives it in advance lest we should rely upon ourselves and not on him alone."

*Half-hearted Christianity halts a marching church.*

*3*

# Keeping the Eyes Open

While the revolution raged in Petrograd in 1917, the Russian Orthodox Church, in session a few blocks away from the fighting, debated heatedly about what color vestments their priests should wear.

The church has always been tempted to avoid conflict rather than get into the middle of it. A church council finds it easier to discuss clogged toilets or the color of tissue in their restrooms than to clarify a moral issue confronting their community. Often neutrality becomes a cave into which we can crawl and watch the world go by. Toleration becomes the pleasant password for not getting involved.

Therefore when Paul urges us to put on the full armor of God we are a bit shocked. It sounds as if a real fight is going on and Paul is serious about us getting into it. Evidently, as Christians, we do not have the option of withdrawal from the struggle. Maybe we thought that we had, in our enlightenment, outgrown devils and demons.

Yet, if we open our eyes, we see that humankind has not been able to subdue the satanic forces. Individuals and nations have been gripped by the hellishness of sin

15

and cannot break free. Our secular, humanistic renaissance has not stopped the rampant march of sin. Our human weapons have been like straw. Our only hope is rescue from the outside. It is the armor provided by God.

In the first place we must ask God to open our eyes to what is happening around us. Albert Speer was a high-ranking official in the Third Reich. He admitted that he was aware of Hitler's anti-Semitic attitude, but he gave it no serious thought. He did not want anything to destroy his idealized picture of Hitler. One day in 1944 Karl Hanke, a government official of Lower Silesia, came to see Speer. He spoke falteringly and told Speer never to accept an invitation to inspect a concentration camp in Upper Silesia. Evidently he had seen something there that was horrifying and that he could not describe. Speer stated that he did not question him; he did not question Himmler; he did not question Hitler. He did not want to know what was happening, even though he secretly thought that Hanke was referring to Auschwitz.

Speer commented in his autobiography, "From that moment on I was inescapably contaminated morally, because from fear of discovering something which might have made me turn from my course I closed my eyes. Because I failed at that time, I still feel responsible for Auschwitz in a wholly personal sense."

Christians must wear the whole armor of God. Otherwise there will be weak spots in our defense that will allow the forces of evil to penetrate. We cannot afford to see only what we want to see! Phillips Brooks said, "There are ten different ways to put out a fire but closing your eyes is not one of them."

And then we must engage in the confrontation. There

is an old movie called *The Hoodlum Priest*. In it, a priest ministers to people in a penitentiary, including one man on death row. The priest and a number of others parade with signs in front of the governor's mansion hoping to grant the prisoner a reprieve from his death sentence. The time for execution comes and goes. The man is killed.

Everyone leaves except the priest. An old policeman comes up to him and says jokingly, "Father, what do you expect to do with that sign? Change the world?"

The priest replies, "No, I don't expect to change the world. I'm just trying to keep the world from changing me."

Keep your eyes open and wear the whole armor of God that you may fight the good fight!

*Evil is not challenged by closed eyes.*

# 4

# Commitment Power

"After you have done everything, to stand" (Eph. 6:13). When Paul urges us to put on the whole armor of God, it is for the purpose of committing ourselves totally to the Lord in the war against evil. He knows what halfhearted allegiance does. He wants us to grow to fullness in Christ. "Then we will no longer be infants tossed back and forth by the waves and blown here and there by every wind of teaching and by the cunning and craftiness of men in their deceitful scheming" (Eph. 4:14).

When are we totally committed to a principle or a person? Let me share with you three little sketches that portray what it means.

The Rev. Mark Jerstad, campus pastor at Augustana College in Sioux Falls, South Dakota, tells of an experience that took place in his senior year at St. Olaf College. Mark was going to the east coast for an interview. He and his girl friend went down to the bus depot early one winter morning and waited for the bus to arrive. When it did and he was ready to hop aboard, Sandy gave him an envelope with a note in it. As the bus headed east, Mark opened it and read the note. It closed with the words, "Yours with the will to love, Sandy."

Love is a mental, volitional choice. It is certainly more than good feelings or sentimental slush. To be lasting there must be the commitment of a resolute act of the will. It is deliberate, persistent goodwill that will push on regardless of circumstances or temporary feelings.

For the second sketch let us travel to Hamar, Norway, where my father grew up as a child. My family and I went there this past summer with our church choir. One afternoon we visited the municipal indoor swimming pool. It was the largest and most luxurious pool I had ever seen. One of our members and I decided to jump off the high board. We challenged each other to dive headfirst. It was a long way down. A bellyflop would be our undoing. But the competition of the challenge left no room for backing down. As I leaped into the air, I thought, "There is no turning back now!" I had to follow through. We read in Scripture, "And if he shrinks back, I will not be pleased with him" (Heb. 10:38).

The third little sketch comes from a *Newsweek* article about tennis star Martina Navratilova. She described her consistently winning formula: "I used to be involved in tennis. Now I am committed. Take ham and eggs— the chicken is involved but the pig is committed."

Committed people change the earth. They are those people who have conviction, an act of will. They are not quitters; they follow through to the end. They are not so afraid of going broke that they are unwilling to go for broke.

This is what Paul desires for the Christian army. He hopes it will always stand fast. We Christians love because God first loved us. We, too, can be committed because God first committed himself to us. Tolstoi, the Russian novelist, was born into the aristocracy. One day he put on old work clothes and went out to work side by side with the peasants. They laughed and joked about it and said, "But this is our lot for life, and you can go back to your royal life whenever you choose." And, of course, he did.

Jesus didn't. He came and slugged it out against evil, went to the cross, rose again, sent us his Spirit, and will come again. He stays with us always and even "if we are faithless, he will remain faithful" (2 Tim. 2:13). Now that is commitment! That is the challenge for the soldier of Christ.

*Ham and eggs: the chicken is involved, but the pig is committed.*

# 5

# *Here I Stand*

Society is on the march. People want progress. Standing still is summed up as monumental defeat. If we are not on the move, we tend to feel guilty.

Several years ago I went raccoon hunting with a friend. It was a brisk October night, and my breath spiraled into the air like smoke. The fallen leaves were a mattress underfoot. The only sounds that sliced through the woods were the hoots of a great horned owl. My friend unleashed his two hounds, and they were off like a flash into the woods. I, too, was waiting to get started.

After several minutes I told my friend, "Let's get going and follow the dogs!"

His reply startled me. "Stand still and keep silent. The dogs are working."

I learned in a hurry that it was no good to rush about until the hounds got the scent of a raccoon and had treed it. Their barking would reveal their find.

There are also times in life when simply standing is significant. In three short verses in Ephesians 6, Paul uses the expressions, "able to stand," and "after you have done everything, to stand," and "stand firm." The

Christian soldier needs to learn the art of defending the fortress as well as launching an assault against the enemy. Before an army can march it may have to learn how to halt. Holding the fort may indeed be a noble thing. If your integrity, your honor, or your home is under siege, you must stand and defend that which you hold dear. Much of the armor that Paul describes for the Christian is for the purpose of warding off the attacks of the evil one.

When you stand fast, you demonstrate to the world your principles and your allegiance. That is good. When you stand for something, you won't fall for everything!

During this past year many have asked me where I stand on such issues as abortion, homosexuality, nuclear arms, and gambling. Their questions have forced me to search the Scriptures, wrestle with my conscience, and then take a stand. The pulpit does not become a place to hide, nor is it big enough to run in. It becomes a place where a minister takes a stand. Every one of us as Christian soldiers needs to stand up and be counted! We need to stand still long enough to build convictions and then defend them.

At the Diet of Worms Martin Luther was asked to repudiate his books and the errors they contained. His answer became immortal: "Unless I am convinced by Scripture and plain reason—I do not accept the authority of popes and councils, for they have contradicted each other—my conscience is captive to the Word of God. I cannot and I will not recant anything, for to go against conscience is neither right nor safe. Here I stand, I cannot do otherwise. God help me. Amen." This was a cry for holding the line.

It is a refreshing thing to have stood your ground while the winds of adversity blew in your face. God gave you strength. You had something to hold on to. Herman Melville said, "A man needs to feel something in this slippery world that holds." In *Markings* Dag Hammarskjöld wrote, "Life only demands from you the strength you possess. Only one feat is possible—not to have run away."

And you did not do it on your own. The giant redwood trees of California are perhaps the largest living things on the earth. You might think they are completely independent. That is not the case. Redwood trees have shallow root systems and grow in groves where their roots intertwine. In this way they support each other so they can stand tall and withstand the storm. Christians also need each other in order "to stand your ground, and after you have done everything, to stand." Remember the words of John Milton when he was totally blind at age 44: "They also serve who only stand and wait."

*Stand for something so you won't fall for everything.*

# 6

# *You Can Depend on Me*

A strong belt or girdle was a necessary part of the attire in the lands of the near east in Jesus' day. Without such girding, the loose flowing garments became cumbersome and hindered the movement of the body. For the soldier the belt was also needed to secure armor and to hold a sword and money bag. The belt kept things from falling apart. Paul tells us that the Christian warriors have truth as their belts or girdles. One's whole nature is held together by integrity.

In the Old Testament the word for truth comes from a verb that means *to be firm, solid, sure*. Its basic meaning is *reliability*. Therefore the Old Testament writers often refer to the "steadfast" love of God. God's love can be trusted. It is not whimsical. Paul reminded Timothy of this when he wrote: "If we are faithless, he will remain faithful for he cannot disown himself" (2 Tim. 2:13).

I once conducted the funeral for a concrete contractor. Following the service, one of those who knew him well said to me. "Al was quite a fellow. His word was always his bond." Truth is not just something in which we are called to believe. We ourselves should *be* truth. No person can be trusted if he or she is honest simply because honesty is a good policy. There are too many situations in life where honesty may not seem the best route to go. As one wit observed, "A lie is an abomination in the eyes of the Lord, but a very present help in time of trouble." Honesty is genuine only when it goes beyond expediency and becomes a matter of total conviction and theology. It was said of Jesus, "The Word became flesh and lived for a while among us. We have seen his glory, the glory of the one and only Son, who came from the Father, full of grace and truth" (John 1:14).

David Livingstone, missionary and explorer, was appalled by the slave trade in Africa. He felt that if Africa had a route from east to west it could be opened up to civilization. So this leader formed a party for an expedition from coast to coast.

Weeks and months passed slowly by as this determined group hacked their way through jungles and swamps. Feats of valor were common in their day-to-day journey. Tsetse flies with their terror of sleeping sickness and mosquitoes whose bites could bring deadly malaria constantly harassed the party. The group passed through villages where a white man's face seemed like a ghostly apparition to the Africans.

Finally they emerged at the port city having surmounted incredible obstacles. Livingstone and the other men in the party were feeble and physically drained. The captain of a large steamer in the harbor told Livingstone, "All England is waiting word from you. They will welcome you with tremendous acclaim. I shall be honored to give you free passage home to England on my steamer."

David Livingstone responded, "These men who accompanied me would then not have the necessary leadership to bring them safely back to their villages. I promised them that if they made this exploration with me, I would guide them home."

The captain and the authorities urged him saying, "There are others who can take your place and bring them home through the unmarked forests. They'll understand. They love you. You are an important man. Your body is worn out, and if you go back into the jungle you may die."

Livingstone made his decision quickly. "I gave them my word and I shall go back into Africa with them."

Truth is not just something we are called to preach. Truth is something we are called to be. "Can you depend on me?" That is a significant question.

*Truth is something you are called to be.*

# 7

# *Open to View*

When I was about 10 years old, I used to enjoy ambling to the cemetery outside my hometown in southwestern Minnesota. It was a fascinating place with tombstones of all sizes and stately trees that stood on sentinel duty. But what lured me out there were the many gophers which claimed the cemetery as their homestead. I would always bring along a pail and some string. An old water pump stood in the middle of the cemetery. I would fill my pail with water and then watch intently until a gopher came up out of its hole. Seeing me, the gopher would run back down the hole, and I would proceed to make a snare with the string, pour water down the hole, and wait for the gopher to pop out of the underground home. Then I would quickly pull the string, and the gopher would be lassoed.

Everything went fine that summer until one day my mother announced that she didn't want me playing around the cemetery. She thought it was disturbing for those who were coming to visit graves or for a burial service to see a boy running around, drowning out gophers. So I took her advice.

However, one day the call of the cemetery was too

appealing for me to refuse. I went out there and caught several gophers. I knew that when I got home mother would ask me as to my whereabouts. Therefore, on the way home from the cemetery I dropped by a friend's house for about half an hour. When I arrived home, mother did ask me where I had been. Quickly I replied, "At my friend's house." Was I truthful? I certainly had been there. At the time I thought I had outwitted my mother. I had done wrong, but I did not think that I had lied.

My conscience did not let me off the hook. Later I told mother "the whole truth, nothing but the truth." Following that I felt relieved and open, as the breeze of honesty freshened my life again.

As the years rolled by and I went to the seminary, I discovered an important thing about the girdle of truth. In the New Testament the word for truth means *non-concealment* or *unhiddenness*. Truth, then, is that which is open to view, expressed rather than suppressed.

Satan has a formidable weapon in deception. We often become disciples of that demeaning device. If someone tells you that you have a call from a person you do not wish to talk to, it is easy to respond, "Say that I'm not here." It may seem like an insignificant thing, but it is a departure from the truth. Someone has said, "Everything that Christians do should be as transparent as sunlight."

Many of us close our letters with the expression, "Sincerely yours." The origin of the word *sincere* is interesting. It comes from two Latin words: *sine*, meaning "without," and *cera*, meaning "wax." So *sincere* means "without wax." The word grew out of the ancient practice of unscrupulous sculptors fraudulently passing off imperfect work with the appearance of perfection. These dishonest workers filled the cracks and blemishes in their marble columns or statues with colored wax. The piece was then buffed, and to the untrained eye the faults were unnoticed. To counter this, the skilled and honest crafts people began labeling their work *sine cere* or "without wax."

The person wearing the girdle of truth should be open to view. There is no need for masks or deception.

*A Christian should be as transparent as sunlight.*

# 8

# *Let Us Not Negotiate*

A little boy was looking at a geography book and made a startling discovery. "Mother, why is it that all the rivers are crooked?" he asked. Mother explained that the water follows the path of least resistance and therefore winds its way around the rocks and heavy clay formations.

Lives often get crooked in the same way. Truth should not be compromised. Paul encourages us to be "girded with truth" because this keeps us on the straight and narrow.

A hunter raised his rifle and took aim at a large bear. When he was about to pull the trigger, the bear spoke in a soft, soothing voice, "Isn't it better to talk than shoot? What do you want? Let us negotiate the matter."

Lowering his rifle the hunter said, "I want a fur coat."

"Good," said the bear. "That is a negotiable question. I want only a full stomach, so let us negotiate a compromise."

They sat down to negotiate, and after a time the bear walked away alone into the dense woods. The negotiations had been successful. The bear had a full stomach, and the devoured hunter had his fur coat.

Satan is deceitful. He often wants us to negotiate the truth of God's commandments. He wants us to believe they are all relative and not absolute. But if truth is negotiated, we violate it.

Daniel was a young man with tremendous potential, a Hebrew boy taken into captivity in Babylon during the exile. He was being trained for a leadership position in the government of King Darius. However, as so often happens, some of the Babylonian officials were envious of the young Hebrew's growing popularity. Therefore they plotted to entrap him. They knew that Daniel prayed regularly to his God. These plotters prevailed on Darius to publish an edict that worship must be offered to no God or person but to the monarch alone, and that when Darius drove forth in his chariot, all people of every rank and station were to prostrate themselves before him. The penalty for refusing to worship the monarch was death at the hands of hungry lions.

On a quiet night Daniel could hear the hoarse roars of the lions as they paced back and forth in their cages. But Daniel did not have to wonder about his decision. It had been made long before when he had decided to always be faithful to his God—no matter what would happen. So Daniel did not change his devotional routine. He did not close his western windows facing Jerusalem. He continued to pray (and be seen), leaving the issue in God's hands.

Daniel received a reprieve from God when he was thrown into the lions' den and their mouths were closed. Deliverance doesn't always happen like that. Some who are faithful to the truth die. However, in so doing they "receive the crown of life." Followers of truth are predictable. They are "straight arrows."

There was another Daniel, who compromised his position and failed to put principle ahead of expediency. He was Daniel Webster, one of the most brilliant of all American orators. Early in life he stood firmly for the abolition of slavery. He called it "a great moral and political evil." But then, like a mirage floating before his eyes, appeared the vision of the White House as a possible goal. He began to hedge on principles and said that while slavery was evil, it was not so great an evil as disunion. He toured the South and was wined and dined. When the final decisions were made for presidential candidates, both the North and the South brushed him aside. When an influential Southerner was asked why they had not supported Webster since he had changed his viewpoint, he sarcastically replied, "The South never pays its slaves."

There are some things that should never be negotiated. Truth is the foremost.

*A straight arrow will fly most accurately.*

# *9*

# *Individual Integrity*

*Chameleon* is a name popularly given to several lizards capable of the seemingly magical maneuver of color transformation. The chameleon looks like a prehistoric monster with a compressed body and a conical head with bulging eyes. It clings to branches with clawed toes and a long grasping tail. The ability of this animal to change colors takes place inside its thick lizard skin. Imagine, if you can, assorted cells like marbles in a jelly substance. Suppose they are yellow, black, and white. If all the yellows crowd to the surface, they will hide the other two colors. The surface appears yellow. The roving eyes of the chameleon are sensitive to certain wavelengths of light, and their signals cause these cells to react in the chameleon's skin. The tiny colored bodies reflect the colors from its surroundings. Thus this remarkable turncoat can blend into many backgrounds.

In a crowd a person can become like a chameleon. Peer pressure often paralyzes the truth within us. When we change colors in order to fit into the background, our convictions slowly die. We become bland. We seldom raise our voices in protest. Conformity becomes the expedient life-style. We are like breakfast food that is guaranteed not to snap, not to crackle, and not to pop. We just lie at the bottom of the bowl and absorb the milk.

We are in trouble if we think more about "what will people say?" than "what will God say?" A church committee member once paraphrased Caesar as he confessed, "I came, I saw, I concurred." Agreeableness is not a good trait when it tampers with truth and justice. Almost every great historic change has been based on nonconformity. The church has been great and pulsating with life when it has been dissatisfied and restless with the world in which it lives. The church has been weak and nonstimulating when it has become comfortable and cozy with the world around it.

We are not to absorb the atmosphere around us but to be transformed by the purified air of the kingdom of God. Martin Luther King Jr. said, "I still believe that standing up for the truth of God is the greatest thing in the world. This is the end of life. The end of life is not to achieve pleasure and avoid pain. The end of life is to do the will of God, come what may."

Truth may sometimes cause you to look peculiar. So be it! Henry Thoreau, a rugged New England individualist of the 19th century, said, "If a man does not keep pace with his companions, perhaps it is because he hears a different drummer. Let him step to the music that he hears, however measured or far away."

Of course, this poses a risk. Truth is not always pleasant. It often upsets the applecart. Hans Christian Andersen told the story of the emperor who was swindled by two tailors who said they would make him some costly robes that would be invisible to those who were not worthy of their positions. No one wanted to tell the truth. Finally when the emperor entered the streets a little boy yelled out, "He has nothing on. The emperor is naked!" Soon the crowd took up the chant.

Never forget the power of truth even though only one voice cries out. Recall the words of Paul: "Don't let the world squeeze you into its own mold, but let God remold your minds from within, so that you may prove in practice that the plan of God for you is good, meets all his demands and moves toward the goal of true maturity" (Rom. 12:2 Phillips).

Don't be a cowering chameleon in hiding. Be bold and not bland as you seek your individual integrity in Christ.

*Discipleship is playing for the coach and not the crowd.*

# Seekers of Truth

"When he, the Spirit of truth, comes, he will guide you into all truth" (John 16:13). Truth is not stagnant, nor is it sterile. As the God of truth goes marching on, so truth is revealed as we follow God. We will never totally arrive at truth until we are transferred to the heavenly kingdom. Paul describes it: "For we know in part. . . . Now we see but a poor reflection" (1 Cor. 13:9, 12). This awareness keeps the Christian soldier humble so he or she will not stumble through arrogance or the know-it-all attitude.

Charles Darwin described the delusion of modern sophistication as being "something like an old hen's knowledge of a 40-acre field, in one corner of which she happens to be scratching."

A little girl came home from school one day with the proud announcement that she had learned the multiplication tables. She had gotten up to 12 times 12. Her grandfather mischievously asked her, "What is 13 times 13?" She replied, "Don't be silly, Grandpa. There is no such thing." There wasn't in her little world of mathematics, but there was in the larger world.

I have always been intrigued by the story of the Wise

Men from the East who came to worship Christ at Bethlehem. We know so little about them. They perhaps did not have the advantage of a written revelation as did the Jews, but they believed that a Redeemer King was to come out of Israel. Imperfect and sketchy as their faith must have been, God honored it and whispered to them the wondrous news of the approaching promise. The whisper was in the form of a star!

Now to me the amazing thing is that they started on such a journey with the meager facts of faith that they possessed. Wouldn't it have been wiser to have waited until the whole Bethlehem event had been better documented?

Yet they saw the star and left all to make the long, dangerous journey to lay worthy gifts at the feet of Jesus. They went to Jesus not to gain something from him, but to give something to him.

In striking contrast to the Wise Men were all those chief priests, high priests, scribes, and other students of Scripture who just sat in their ivory towers. They had the knowledge, but it was merely formal. Their doctrine was dead and did not arouse them from their stupor. They were "balcony types," endlessly discussing and debating the mysteries of God, stewing and brewing over the pros and cons of religion.

The Wise Men were "girded with truth." Truth was their traveling garment as they followed revelation. The religious leaders of that day tried to keep the truth enclosed in a book, and they never saw truth served up in walking papers.

Walter Luthi said, "Stop all this chattering about Christ and take one little step, however diffident or even laughably small it may be, along His path. One inch in this direction is worth more than a thousand miles of discussion about Him."

For the Wise Men scanty truth led to greater truth as their longing souls led them to the baby in a manger who was "full of grace and truth." The Christian is a pilgrim and a traveler. Truth in every realm must be searched out.

George Gallup Jr. says that in our day there is a continuing anti-intellectual strain in our religious life. He asks, "Is religion in the United States a blend of religion of the mind and the heart, or is it degenerating into sterile intellectualism on the one hand or empty emotionalism on the other?" On either extreme the Christian soldier is vulnerable, easy prey for false prophets.

John Shelby, the Episcopal bishop of Newark, writes, "I'm convinced that the only authentic defense of the faith involves honest scholarship. . . . Nothing less than this seems worthy of Christians."

*In pursuit of truth you never travel in vain.*

# 11

# The Protection of Purity

In order to keep them free of disease-carrying bacteria, restaurants are periodically checked by health inspectors. Cleanliness is crucial. If you have an open wound on your body, it does no good to cover it with a bandage unless the wound has first been cleansed. The best protection against infection is having the surrounding area scrubbed up.

The best protection in preserving your life from the onslaughts of evil is having a pure heart.

Paul tells the church at Ephesus that they should wear the "breastplate of righteousness." The soldier of that day wore a breastplate or a coat of mail to protect the vital organs, especially the heart. Right living is the most powerful way of keeping wrong out of your life.

In the Beatitudes, Jesus says, "Blessed are the pure in heart, for they will see God" (Matt. 5:8). The word *pure* occurs 28 times in the New Testament. Ten times it is translated "clean." When it is used with linen, it means white linen; with gold, unalloyed; with glass, clear glass. Rightness of mind and singleness of motive seem to be two dominant themes of the word's intent.

Many people scoff at purity. Who wants to be a

"goody-goody"? Rather be one of the boys, or one of the girls. We have overreacted to the days of strict puritanism. Many disdain a moralistic type of sermon. "Don't make it a moral issue," we hear. Divorce, extra-marital affairs, living arrangements outside marriage, drugs, deceit, public profanity, and a host of other immoral missiles are flying high these days. And they are tolerated and sometimes applauded as the signs of liberated people.

It is said that Mark Twain often began his lectures by introducing himself in the third person. He would say, "I don't know much about this man. At least I know only two things about him: one is, he has never been in the penitentiary; and the other is, I don't know why he hasn't." We think such a statement is clever. We would like to keep both God and our sin. The only problem is that it won't work. They don't mix!

Matthew Arnold said that *chastity* and *charity* were marks of early Christianity. Chastity was not only sexual purity but also decency and integrity. It was a winning virtue as it released a pagan world from the bondage of lust and cruelty. Righteousness includes both chastity and charity. It is the breastplate that protects the heart and keeps it pure. The promise attached to the pure is superb—"for they shall see God."

A little boy once had his hand caught in his mother's expensive narrow-necked vase. He was unable to pull it out. His mother saw his dilemma and noticed that his hand was balled up in a fist. So she told her son to open his hand inside the vase and that would make it narrower so it would slip out more easily. "Oh, no!" the youngster sobbed. "Then I'd lose my marble."

Adults are just as foolish. They want the gifts of God such as peace, pardon, and power—but they don't want to let go of the "marble" in their hands. That marble may be an illicit relationship or perhaps the love of money. Whatever it is, it stands between them and God. Then there is no breastplate of righteousness, and a person is vulnerable to many other attacks by Satan.

Sin blinds and binds and ends in bitterness. Righteousness frees and fortifies and ends in fulfillment. Morality is a breastplate. It is never going to be outdated or outmoded. James simply states it: "Religion that God our Father accepts as pure and faultless is this: to look after orphans and widows in their distress, and to keep oneself from being polluted by the world" (James 1:27).

*You see best through clean glasses.*

# 12

# By This Sign, Conquer

The Roman emperor Constantine the Great, before a battle at Milvian Bridge, is said to have had a vision of the cross appearing in the noonday sky together with the legend written in Latin, "By this sign, conquer!" According to the story, this vision moved Constantine to adopt the Christian religion.

Many horror movies depict vampires or demonic persons attacking an innocent victim. The person seems doomed, but suddenly finds a cross and holds it out, thus warding off the attacker, who is driven away by the sight of the cross.

Perhaps the world has often thought of the cross as an amulet or charm that will protect the wearer or the holder of it. Certainly the cross was never meant to be a lucky rabbit's foot. It was also not meant to be a battle emblem that would guarantee victory to the armies that held it aloft. But there is power in the cross of Christ. It is the redemptive, reconciling power that comes through the atonement of Christ.

When I was a boy, I lived in a fairly rigid Christian community. There were many things on the taboo list. Any movie in a theater was wrong. The pool hall was the residence of the devil. Dancing always spelled damnation. In such an environment the conscience carried a load of guilt. Even when real sin was confessed, it was not buried. The burden of guilt was still carried, even though Christ had taken it upon himself on the cross.

When we feel burdened by guilt, we need to understand the breastplate of righteousness. In essence it is the cross of Christ. It can quiet our condemning consciences and free the spirit of joy. We know that we are saved by grace and it is not of our own doing (Eph. 2:8-9). We understand that we do not get right with God, but that we are put right with God through the cross of Jesus Christ. Some days we might not feel up to par spiritually, but we are still accepted by God and have not been abandoned by him. If Satan accuses us of sin that we have confessed penitently to God, we can tell Satan to be on his way, because the sin has been dealt with and there are no charges against us. We can show him the cross.

A pastor answers the question "Are you saved?" with the reply, "Yes, and I can name the day and the hour. The day was Good Friday, and the hour three o'clock in the afternoon." The atonement was an event. In that sense salvation is an event too. This does not mean universal salvation. It does mean that when salvation is accepted, whether in Baptism, adult conversion, or whatever, it is God's doing and the salvation event is complete.

Paul had a lot of garbage from his past. It could have haunted him forever. But he wore the breastplate of righteousness. He held the cross in front of him. It was adequate. He said, ". . . not having a righteousness of my own that comes from the law, but that which is through faith in Christ—the righteousness that comes from God and is by faith" (Phil. 3:9).

Wars of the spirit will continue. Satan sets his snares with great regularity. He wants to throw us off balance so we doubt our faith. He wants to trap us into thinking we have not measured up and that God's salvation is lacking something. In the Protestant tradition, we may have lost the art of making the sign of the cross. Perhaps we should revive the practice. For it reminds me of that cross of Christ which is my protective breastplate. By that cross I will conquer life and death!

*The cross is not an amulet but an armor.*

# 13

# Watch Your Weak Points

My oldest son is in police work. When on duty, he wears a bulletproof vest to protect his vital organs. It is the smart thing to do, because a criminal who attacks with a gun will probably shoot for the points of vulnerability in the chest region.

In the world of sports a coach endeavors to find the weak points of the opposition and then tries to take advantage of that. In football when a rookie comes in for a play on defense, you will often see the ball run or thrown his way. In basketball the coach will try to send in a taller player against a smaller one to get the dominance. In boxing each fighter tries to exploit the other's weakness.

The Great Wall of China is a huge structure, built long ago at tremendous cost of time and labor. When it was constructed, in the third century before Christ, it seemed to be the final answer to the problem of security. But within a few years the wall was breached three times, not by soldiers making an assault upon the thick stone and masonry wall, but by enemies who bribed the gatekeepers. A lack of integrity among the guards was the point of vulnerability.

In Satan's war against the human soul we can expect the same approach. Satan will attack us at our weak points. We are told, "Be self-controlled and alert. Your enemy the devil prowls around like a roaring lion looking for someone to devour" (1 Peter 5:8). Therefore Paul encourages us to wear the breastplate of righteousness. A righteous life is our best protection. Periodic checks need to be made on our lives to see if there are some cracks in our armor.

A city water company circulated information about the high cost of neglecting to check household leaks in the plumbing system. In order to portray the facts graphically, a tiny circle only one thirty-second of an inch in diameter was printed. Opposite the circle appeared the information that through even so small a hole 6,550 gallons of water would escape in a month's time. Another circle, one-sixteenth of an inch in diameter would permit 26,230 gallons of water to escape in a month. Finally, opposite a circle one-fourth of an inch in diameter was the information that through such a hole 375,150 gallons would be lost in one month. Small leaks are costly.

It is the same way in human life. We often overlook little flaws or sins, explaining them away as just human nature. Certainly they are nothing to get excited about. We forget that evil is evil in whatever degree it is found. And unless checked, evil will always grow in scope and intensity. Satan will always try to pry into our lives through those little leaks and flaws whose magnitude we are prone to minimize. Evil can then flood the landscape of the soul.

In discovering our points of vulnerability we need

to survey our lives with the binoculars of the Bible. Sometimes we will also need the scutinizing eye of a friend, for we often cannot see ourselves with discriminating eyes. When my children were small, I saw an example of how we see wrongs in others and miss them in ourselves. Before we prayed at meals, I told the children to fold their hands and close their eyes. One morning at breakfast our little daughter, Debbie, exclaimed with a detective's glee as we were praying, "Daddy, Barak is not closing his eyes!"

I asked Debbie, "How do you know that Barak's eyes were not closed?"

Sheepishly she realized that what she accused in her brother was her own undoing.

Dag Hammarskjöld wrote: "You cannot play with the animal in you without becoming wholly animal, play with falsehood without forfeiting your right to truth, play with cruelty without losing your sensitivity of mind. He who wants to keep his garden tidy doesn't reserve a plot for weeds." A breastplate of righteousness protects the soil of the soul from the weeds of evil.

*Life's resources are spoiled by erosion of soil and soul!*

# 14

# The Rightness of Righteousness

As you drive through the flat plains states of our country, you will notice that in some areas long belt-lines of trees and shrubs have been planted. They were planted to curb the effects of the winds that would scrape off the thin topsoil and send it sailing in the sky to other regions. These rows of vegetation also provide shelter for wildlife. In hilly country, trees are planted to keep the soil from washing down the steep banks when torrential rains fall. The root system will hold the precious soil in place.

The planting system reminds me of an important truth about my Christian life. The business of planting the trees of goodness should occupy more of my time than hunting for weeds. "It is better to light a candle than curse the darkness." That is solid advice. It sometimes seems easier to get people to march in a crusade *against* something than to get them to stand up *for* something.

If you have adjacent rooms connected by a doorway, you may want to try an experiment. Turn on bright lights in one room. Close the door to the adjacent room which is in total darkness. Now open the door. What happens? Does the darkness sneak into the lighted room? Not at all. The light travels into the dark room, and the lighted room remains bright. Life is that way.

Today demands deeds of love and concern from the people of God. Principles enunciated and hopes expressed are not enough. The best way to fight evil is with positive, affirmative action and not with negative haranguings. In this game of Christian strategy the best defense is a good offense. An old pastor once said, "The best way to fight Satan is to serve the Lord."

When you fill your mind and your life with good things, there will be little opportunity for bad thoughts to creep in and get an audience. That is why Paul exhorts us: "Finally, brothers, whatever is true, whatever is noble, whatever is right, whatever is pure, whatever is lovely, whatever is admirable—if anything is excellent or praiseworthy, think about such things" (Phil. 4:8).

If your lawn is filled with crabgrass or some other obnoxious weeds, you could get down on your hands and knees and spend a lifetime trying to root it all out. Or you could prepare the soil, plant good seed, fertilize it, and allow the good grass to crowd out the bad. Life will work that way, too. Paul says, "Do not be overcome by evil, but overcome evil with good" (Rom. 12:21).

Now this style of life does not guarantee immunity from adversity. The opposite may be true. Light exposes the darkness, and the darkness doesn't like it at all. George MacLeod once complained that there is nothing in the modern church that makes the world want to crucify it. That may be putting it a bit strong, but we do know that when we have become adjusted to the world we are largely ignored by it. A comment made about the early church was that they "caused trouble all over the world" (Acts 17:6). Often in our society there are no longer sharp lines drawn between the Christian and the non-Christian. In such a situation there is less danger of persecution, but perhaps a greater danger of losing one's own soul.

One of the beatitudes is, "Blessed are those who are persecuted because of righteousness, for theirs is the kingdom of heaven" (Matt. 5:10). Again and again the great advances of the Christian faith have come when righteousness was willing to go even to a cross.

During the Reformation in England, Hugh Latimer was burned at the stake. Latimer saw the burning sticks as a light that would shine far beyond the moment and the place of his burning. He reportedly turned and said to his companion in death: "Be of good comfort, Master Ridley, and play the man; we shall this day light such a candle in England as I trust shall never be put out."

*Accentuating the positive does eliminate the negative.*

# 15

# One Man's Swan Song

Henry Francis Lyte had a lifelong wish that he might write

Some simple strain, some spirit-moving lay,
Some sparklet of the soul that still might live
When I was passed to clay.

He was born in Scotland, June 1, 1793, and was early left an orphan. He struggled through poverty, and by sheer persistence he attended college. On three occasions this gentle soul won prizes in poetry.

His first dream was to become a physician, but his pathway led into the ministry. A turning point in the depth of his ministry happened when he was called to the bedside of a friend who was dying. Neither man seemed able to cope with the inevitable ending of it all. They prayed and studied Scripture together until faith solidified and gave them both a firm foundation for hope in life and in death. Lyte wrote of this friend: "He died happy under the belief that though he had deeply erred, there was One whose death and sufferings would atone for his delinquencies, and that he was forgiven and accepted for His sake."

This experience warmed his heart and spilled over into his preaching. For nearly 25 years Lyte labored among the humble fisherfolk and sailors of the parish of Lower Brixham. Because of frail health he found it necessary to spend some winters in a more favorable climate. In the fall of 1847 he wrote to a friend that the swallows were flying southward, and he observed, "They are inviting me to accompany them; and yet alas; while I am talking of flying, I am just able to crawl."

The time came for his farewell service. Some parishioners thought he was too weak to preach and serve Communion. But his indomitable spirit would not listen to that. He wanted to wear out rather than rust out.

After the service the exhausted Lyte walked out along the ocean shoreline and watched the splendor of the setting sun in a glory of crimson and gold. It was a magnificent evening. Pastor Lyte seemed to have a premonition that it was also the evening of his life. He trudged home and went into his study. An hour passed. He came out of his study and handed a manuscript to a relative. It was September 4, 1847, and in the heat of inspiration he had written what was to become one of Christendom's most favorite hymns, "Abide with Me."

The first and last verses of the hymn are these:

Abide with me, fast falls the eventide.
The darkness deepens; Lord, with me abide.
When other helpers fail and comforts flee,
Help of the helpless, oh, abide with me.

Hold thou thy cross before my closing eyes,
Shine through the gloom, and point me to the skies;

Heav'n's morning breaks, and earth's vain shadows
  flee;
In life, in death, O Lord, abide with me.

He was protected by the breastplate of righteousness.
Fear could not penetrate his soul because of Christ's pardon given to him. "And be found in him, not having a righteousness of my own that comes from the law, but that which is through faith in Christ—the righteousness that comes from God and is by faith" (Phil. 3:9).

*When you know how to die, you know how to live.*

# 16

# Pulling the Punches

An important work of the peacemaker is the practice of self-restraint. Much strife is caused by those who say what they think or feel, without regard to the hurt or damage it may inflict on others. The person whose feet are "fitted with the readiness that comes from the gospel of peace" will apply self-restraint in conversation and conduct.

Recently I watched a brutal boxing match. One of the fighters was being pummeled and pounded around the ring by the fury of the other far-superior boxer. Toward the end of the fight the battered man was susceptible to every jab that came his direction. However, one thing was noticeable. The dominant boxer was pulling his punches. He eased up on the attack. He did not want to seriously injure his opponent. It was an act of sportsmanship in an otherwise violent sport. Self-restraint was being exercised.

Most of us are reactors. When rubbed the wrong way, we retaliate or reciprocate in like manner. George Bernard Shaw once sent Winston Churchill two tickets to the opening of a play, and said in the note attached: "Bring a friend, if you have one."

Churchill wrote back, "It is impossible for me to attend the opening of your play, but I'll attend the second night, if you have one."

In our homes there is always the testing of each other that makes the peace fly into pieces. Judith Viorst interviews children. One of the stories went like this: "My mommy got so mad," said Megan, "she yanked the plate off the table and the mashed potatoes flew into the air." She was asked why a mother would ever do a thing like that. "Well," Megan continued, "she told my brother to eat his potatoes, and Mike said, 'Soon.' Then she told him to eat his potatoes, and Mike said, 'In a minute.' And then she told him again. Mike responded, 'How can I eat them? They're cold.' "

Surely we all have breaking points when we reach the end of our string, but as we grow older the string ought to become longer.

When I was a boy, I used to listen to the radio comedy team Amos and Andy. Once Amos purposed to get even with one of his friends who was always slapping him across the chest. Amos announced to Andy that he was ready for him. "I've put a stick of dynamite in my vest pocket," he said. "The next time he slaps me on the chest, he'll get his hand blown off." Amos failed to see that the same charge would blow his own heart out.

Judas led a group of soldiers into the Garden of Gethsemane, where he betrayed Jesus. When those with Jesus saw what was happening, one drew his sword and struck the slave of the high priest and cut off his right ear. But Jesus touched his ear and healed him. Jesus gave the warning, "Put your sword back in its place, for all who draw the sword will die by the sword" (Matt. 26:52).

When we do not practice self-restraint, the vicious cycle always goes on. An uncontrolled outburst is followed by another. Hatred and hostility always boomerang. A wise writer of Proverbs knew human experience when he wrote, "A gentle answer turns away wrath, but a harsh word stirs up anger" (Prov. 15:1).

Jesus took the punches of people without striking back. He broke the chain reaction of people wounding one another. Jesus was a shock absorber. His epitaph could well read: "The hurt stops here."

Paul tells us, "For God did not give us a spirit of timidity, but a spirit of power, of love, and of self-discipline" (2 Tim. 1:7). A peacemaker needs self-discipline.

*Be an actor rather than a reactor.*

# 17

# Bridges and Fences

A peacemaker is just that—a maker of peace. The word *shalom* is a rich part of the Jewish vocabulary. It is a greeting used by Jewish people all over the world. The Hebrew word for peace, it means more than the absence of evil and strife. It is a wish for all the good things that contribute to happiness. The peacemaker thus gives himself or herself to the creation of positive goodwill. The apostle Paul illustrates this in a word of advice to the Christians in Rome. "Do not be overcome by evil, but overcome evil with good" (Rom. 12:21). This type of behavior calls for imagination and resourcefulness.

The great preacher Wallace Hamilton told of an Indiana sheep raiser who had a real problem. His neighbors' dogs were killing his sheep. When this continued for some time, it became apparent that something had to be done. What should be his course of action? He could have brought a lawsuit, which most people think of first. He could have shot or poisoned his neighbors' dogs, since they were trespassing. He could have built more and better fences, which would have been very costly. But he didn't do any of these things. He had a better idea. To each of his neighbors' children he gave a lamb or two as pets. In time, when all the neighbors had their own small flocks, they began to tie up their dogs, and that put an end to the matter.

Fences or bridges? That is often the question. An old slogan says that "good fences make good neighbors." There is some truth to that if you have wandering cows. But in the area of the spirit it is not true. Fences keep people out, and they keep you in.

Bridges are built for the opposite purpose. They allow people to cross over to one another. They provide accessibility. The people of peace are bridge builders and not fence makers.

It is easy to fan the ashes of ancient feuds. It is difficult to create understanding and harmony. Peace never just comes, because human nature is real and its trademark is alienation. Jesus made peace by giving his life on a cruel cross. Paul talks about the bridge building of Jesus: "But now in Christ Jesus you who once were far away have been brought near through the blood of Christ. For he himself is our peace, who has made the two one and has destroyed the barrier of hostility, by abolishing in his flesh the law with its commandments and regulations. His purpose was to create in himself one new man out of the two, thus making peace, and in this one body to reconcile both of them to God through the cross, by which he put to death their hostility. He came and preached peace to you who were far away and peace to those who were near. For through him we both have access to the Father by one Spirit" (Eph. 2:13-18).

The person who wears the sandals of peace always has reconciliation foremost in the mind. Reconciliation to

God and to each other is the fundamental task. At times the sandals of peace move with gentleness and at times step with sternness. But they always attempt to avoid the path of provocation. Augustine characterized his mother, Monica, with these words: "She shewed herself such a peacemaker, that hearing on both sides most bitter things, . . . she never would disclose aught of the one unto the other, but what might tend to their reconcilement."

In a world of strife and war, Jesus calls us to find peace by making peace.

*Peace is not found; it is made.*

# 18

# Singing the Right Song

The Greeks had a story to illustrate the power of positive goodness to drive out the negative force of evil. It was about the sirens that sang so sweetly that sailors, hearing their music, could not resist the temptation to go toward them. This always brought the sailors to their destruction. Finally, however, they solved their problem. They put better music on the ship than that which came from the sirens outside. When Orpheus sang, the sirens lost their appeal.

Many songs have been emitted from the church. When the main theme is doom and the melody is dull, the assembled congregation is not stirred to service. When the songs dance and sparkle with life, the people are persuaded to celebrate the goodness of God. If the music on board the good ship church is no better than the sirens of our day on the outside, we are in trouble!

The music that we are talking about is not just a hymn or an organ composition, but rather the tempo and topic of our entire worship. As Paul catalogs the armor of the Christian army he tells us that we must march, "With your feet fitted with the readiness that comes from the gospel of peace" (Eph. 6:15). This certainly indicates that our movement is not characterized by damnation denunciations or heavy-handed judgments. There is a lightness in the step, gentleness and joy. It is a celebrative, creative cadence. Paul says, "How beautiful are the feet of those who bring good news!" (Rom. 10:15).

The song of the soldier of Christ is a song of peace that comes from the pardon and power of Jesus. As Jesus appeared to his disciples following the resurrection, he said to them, "Peace be with you! As the Father has sent me, so I am sending you. . . . Receive the Holy Spirit. If you forgive anyone his sins, they are forgiven" (John 20:21-23).

Forgiveness leads to peace. You will not be able to wear the shoes of peace without experiencing the joys and deliverance of forgiveness. Alvin Rogness once asked a Buddhist priest what the major difference was between Christianity and Buddhism. The priest quickly replied, "The forgiveness of sin." This is the major chord of the marching music of the church.

I have made many trips to the Bighorn Mountains of Wyoming. We know a rancher there who permits us to hunt on his land. He has cattle grazing in the mountain valleys and on the high plateaus. There is one thing he is concerned about when we hunt there. When we go through a gate, he wants us to be sure to close it immediately after passing through. He does not want his cattle to get out and wander into the forest or pastures of neighboring ranchers. We always heed his words of warning, "Be sure to close the gates behind you!"

This is exactly what God does for me. He closes the gate on my yesterdays so that past sins cannot break into my today. They are forgiven and forgotten. He gives me a fresh start and a new song every morning.

And then Jesus requests me to do the same to my neighbor. There ought to be no ledger-keeping of my neighbor's wrongs. Grudges should be dropped at the close of the day. When the gate is consciously closed, the irritations cannot wander from one pasture to another. Peace comes walking softly on the heels of forgiveness. For "In him we have redemption through his blood, the forgiveness of sins" (Eph. 1:7). That is the right song to sing and will keep us from following the seducing sirens!

*At the end of the day, close the gate.*

# 19

# Walking in Hush Puppies

We have always had animals around our family set-ting. When my children were young, we owned a pet goat. He was a nice little kid, but as he grew older he became very mischievous. One night he tore his chain loose and the next morning was nowhere to be found. When we located him, we found he had gotten tangled up on a neighbor's porch where he had eaten some plants and left his droppings on the floor. Needless to say, we advertised a goat "for free" in the daily newspaper. Someone called about him much sooner than expected. As the man was leading him into his pickup truck he smiled and said, "Now I can tell my neighbors that I got the pastor's goat!"

That expression of getting someone's goat has an inter-esting history. In the early days of horse racing the own-ers would use goats to calm down their high-strung horses. Having a goat in the stall with the horse was like having a tranquilizer. When someone would try to fix a race so that a certain horse would not win, he would steal the goat from the horses's stall. The horse would then become nervous and irritable. Out of this situation the expression was born, "He got my goat." The person was left angry and disagreeable.

The Christian soldier is not out to get someone's goat. Paul says we should come to someone wearing the sandals of peace. We are not called to stir up a situation but to settle one down. When I wear my cowboy boots you can hear me coming down the hallway and it draws attention to me. When I come in tennis shoes there is little sound and little attraction. The Christian travels with padded feet, walking softly in Hush Puppies, for a Christian is a bringer of peace and not provocation.

There is a sensitivity about those who walk softly. They trample neither the flowers nor the feelings of others. They hear what is going on, because their own footsteps do not drown out the sounds of the world around them.

At times, of course, Jesus came marching into a situation with warrior boots. Judgment could be heard in his footsteps. In his vision John says, "His feet were like bronze glowing in a furnace" (Rev. 1:15). This was true when Jesus marched into Jerusalem and cleansed the temple by overturning the money tables and driving out the racketeers. Most often, however, we see Jesus walking serenely into a situation with sandals of peace.

There is a beautiful illustration of this when Jesus and his disciples came upon the woman of Samaria at the well (John 4). Jesus justly told her of her errors both in morals and theology. He did it in a way that caused no needless embarrassment. He did not make her cringe with caustic remarks about her past behavior. Jesus was so aware of her predicament—her loss of dignity, her ostracism from society—that he wasn't going to trample on the wilting flower of her life. She was there at the well at noon because she could not stand the gossip and the glances of the women of the community who came there in the shade of the day.

Jesus, knowing all this, sent the 12 disciples into town to buy food. This was certainly the height of inefficiency. I am sure Jesus did this because he wanted to talk to the woman alone. He knew she would be uptight with 12 men sitting around with eager ears. The conversation would not have gotten off the ground in a crowd. Out of a private, caring conversation came a conversion from sinner to saint!

That is the way Jesus moved. He silently met Nicodemus at night, for he was aware that at his stage in the spiritual pilgrimage Nicodemus did not want to compromise his standing among the Pharisees. Jesus avoided causing further embarrassment to the woman taken in adultery, yet plainly told her, "Do not sin again." Without causing a stir, he met the needs of the wedding couple at Cana when their wine ran out. Where he walked, a fragrance was left on his path. John says, "Whoever claims to live in him must walk as Jesus did" (1 John 2:6). It is like walking softly in Hush Puppies of peace.

*A Christian's walk is marked by footprints of peace.*

# 20

# Gamblers for Peace

One of the crowning indignities heaped on Jesus in the tragic hours before the crucifixion occurred when the soldiers dressed him up in a scarlet robe, put a reed in his hand, and placed a crown of thorns on his head. Some translators describe the robe as a general's short crimson cloak. What irony this was to make the Prince of Peace wear the trappings of a warlord.

Subsequent generations have also been guilty of dressing up Jesus in the uniforms of their making. Militarists have put him in khaki green. Clergy have dressed him in exquisite liturgical finery. Business has put him in the pin-striped suit of a high-powered executive.

We need to go back to the Gospels and let Jesus stand out unhindered and undisguised. There his first priority was to establish peace, and so we must recognize Jesus in that light. He did not play on people's passions and hatred. He always tried to stir up sympathy and good will. He fought evil but loved the evildoers. We often do the opposite; we fight the evildoers and then keep the evil. We kill the warriors and then preserve the war system.

Therefore we must constantly reappraise our strategy

to see if we are marching in keeping with Jesus' style with having our "feet fitted with the readiness that comes from the gospel of peace." One of the striking facts described in Barbara Tuchman's *The Guns of August* is the stupidity of the French generals, who were so intent on their own fixed plan of attack that they could not believe reports from their own scouts about the movements of German troops, reports which should have caused them to alter radically their own strategy. They were blind to the truth that might have saved them.

We still seem to think that force is the only combatant against force. We are reluctant to believe that reconciliation may work. Of course, if you offer the olive branch of peace, you might get it knocked out of your hand. You may get set back on your heels when the fragrance of forgiveness is on your breath. But in spite of that, God's truth declares that the peacemaker is the ultimate winner. What if some battles are lost when the war is won! Jesus was nailed to the cross when he refused to find refuge in the legions of heaven to come and deliver him. Yet he said, "But I, when I am lifted up from the earth, will draw all men to myself" (John 12:33).

In order to be people of peace, we need to be great gamblers. There is risk involved for individuals and nations. In the play *The Detective* a priest is concerned about the possible reclamation of an unidentified, skillful thief who steals precious art and always makes good his escape. At one point the priest disobeys his bishop's directive. Instead of sending a rare jewel-encrusted cross across France with armed guards, the priest carries it himself with no protection. The thief, Flambeau, appears, steals the cross, and escapes. When the bishop calls the priest to account for his disobedience, the priest replies, "I gambled the cross for a man's soul, trusting that ultimately both could be recovered." That is what God did at Calvary. He asks us to do the same!

Many have thought they could destroy the church and its message. One big push and it would topple. History has proven otherwise. For the church is the body of Christ, and he is Lord forever. Let us remember the words of Theodore Beza to the 16th century king of Navarre who thought he could send the church reeling by his blows: "Sire, it is the lot of the church in whose name I speak to receive blows, not to inflict them. But it may please your majesty to remember that the church is an anvil which has worn out many hammers."

The road of the peacemaker may be rough, but the Christian's sandals of peace are sturdy enough for the journey.

*The road may be rough, but the sandals of peace will not wear out.*

# 21

# *A Filtering Faith*

Did faith shelter Paul from the rain of adversity? Did faith provide him with a rose garden whose walls secured him against the maraudings of beast or robber? If you think Paul led a protected life, listen to this catalog of events: "Five times I received from the Jews the forty lashes minus one. Three times I was beaten with rods, once I was stoned, three times I was shipwrecked, I spent a night and a day in the open sea, I have been constantly on the move. I have been in danger from rivers, in danger from bandits, in danger from my own countrymen, in danger from Gentiles; in danger in the city, in danger in the country, in danger at sea; and in danger from false brothers. I have labored and toiled and have often gone without sleep; I have known hunger and thirst and have often gone without food; I have been cold and naked. Besides everything else, I face daily the pressure of my concern for all the churches" (2 Cor. 11:24-28).

We might conclude that Paul would have received poor grades in learning the art of wielding the shield of faith. It certainly appears that he didn't use it properly, since so many devastating darts hit him squarely between the eyes. But maybe we are prone to think that way because we have misinterpreted the promises of the Lord. Perhaps the shield of faith is not an umbrella that keeps us cozy and blocks out all calamity. We have often wanted a shield that would protect us from pain, box out bereavement, preserve our possessions, contain our comfortableness, and prosper our pleasure. And since the shield of faith fails to do all this, we are often stunned and confused and wonder where it all went wrong.

Paul saw the shield of faith in a different light. It was not to prevent all ill circumstances, but it was a shield to keep ill circumstances from doing him harm. His body might be buffeted, but his soul would be saved. Paul had a shield of faith that would prevent him from being impoverished in the wealth of his soul.

A ray of white light is made up of many colors. We can devise a screen to divert or keep back any of these colors and to let through those we please. There are screens that will permit rays of light to come through but will keep out rays of heat. We can intercept certain rays and forbid their presence. The apostle Paul used the shield of faith in this way. He put it in this way, "I have learned to be content whatever the circumstances. I know what it is to be in need, and I know what it is to have plenty. I have learned the secret of being content in any and every situation, whether well fed or hungry, whether living in plenty or in want. I can do everything through him who gives me strength" (Phil. 4:11-13). Faith was the shield that enabled Paul to intercept the deadly darts of evil that can dwell in all circumstances.

We need a shield of faith not to guarantee that we will never fail, but that in failure we will be protected from pessimism that paralyzes the soul from trying again. We need a shield that in the face of injury we do not give birth to a spirit of revenge. In the face of pain we do not want to wallow in self-pity and complaint. In the winds of disappointment we do not want to cringe in cynicism. In the confrontation of a great challenge we desire to be guarded from cowardice. When success comes in at full tide, we need the shield that snuffs out deadly vanity and self-conceit.

Erskine Mason once said, "If you cannot bring your condition to your mind, bring your mind to your condition."

Perhaps this is what a man did who was suffering from an illness. A friend asked him, "This dreadful condition you find yourself in must certainly have colored your life."

His reply was simple and courageous. "Yes," he replied, "but I chose the color."

The shield of faith in Jesus Christ filters out the deadly rays of evil.

*Faith does not shield from calamity but from cowardice.*

# 22

# Seventeen to Nothing

A man was passing a field in which some young boys were playing baseball. Sidling up to a lad in the outfield, the man asked, "What is the score?"

"Seventeen to nothing, sir," the boy replied.

"Well, which side is ahead?" the man asked.

"They are," the boy said.

"That looks pretty bad for you, doesn't it?" was the question.

The confident youngster smiled and stated, "Oh, no, sir, it ain't so bad. We ain't been up to bat yet!"

It seems at times that the score is "17 to nothing" against peace, against morals, against mercy and righteousness. We may have had a turn at the plate, but we have not gotten on base. The game has become a laugher, and darkness descends on the field of play. Have the odds of winning dwindled to the impossible? History has been dotted with agonizing situations. The forces of darkness have held the upper hand against the troops of light. And then, God puts a star in the sky. There is another inning to play! Another chance at bat!

It happened when the star of Bethlehem restored hope. It started with a small baby in a manger. But the box could not contain him as he "grew and became strong; he was filled with wisdom, and the grace of God was upon him" (Luke 2:40). The mighty Christ stepped up to the plate with the bat of righteousness and with a mighty swing hit a bases-loaded homer of redemption. Again he stepped up and scored a resurrection run. The game was changed around, and the sky was lighted with glory and hope.

The game has continued down through the innings of the centuries. It appears that the light has lost its advantage. What will happen now? We do not know what the next inning has in store for us. With half-knowledge we live in uncertainties, mysteries, doubts. We look again at the scoreboard and tremble. Is it a lost cause?

Then we raise the shield of faith. God has not left the ball field. He places the bat in the hands of the Christian church and empowers his people with his Spirit. This allows us to take our eyes off the scoreboard and center our attention on the field of play. That is where it should be.

There is an old saying: "Where there is no faith in the future, there is no power in the present." The faith-life enables us to contemplate the whole game rather than the single inning. One inning may seem to go against us, but faith knows that one inning is not the end of the game or the world. "You will grieve, but your grief will turn to joy" (John 16:20). Faith takes the long view, the view of the entire campaign. "I saw the Holy City, the new Jerusalem, coming down out of heaven from God" (Rev. 21:2). "The kingdom of the world has become the kingdom of our Lord and of his Christ, and he will reign for ever and ever" (Rev. 11:15). Such a relationship to the Lord protects our life with an invincible shield.

In a dramatic way the shield of faith protects our attitude. It transforms us from whiners to winners. Rather than cursing darkness we light the candle. We don't look for a place to hide but rather for a place to play the game of faith. In June 1940, Winston Churchill flew to Tours, France, and upon returning called a special session of the British War Cabinet. He announced to his dismayed ministers that France was on the verge of caving in and asking Hitler for his terms. He painted the situation in the grimmest colors. He reviewed the desperate military and political outlook and summed it up by saying, "We are now facing Germany completely isolated. We are alone." The room was filled with foreboding silence. Churchill, who was then 66 years of age, looked into the blank faces surrounding him and said, "I find it rather inspiring." The confidence of their leader lifted the drooping spirits of England as they rose to meet the challenge of their day.

This same spirit must be foremost in the Christian family in this hour as we triumphantly sing, "Lead on, O King eternal!" Through faith we confront our day with confidence!

*No faith in the future—no power in the present.*

# 23

# *Defeating Discouragement*

One of the most devastating darts the devil throws our way is discouragement. When it runs its full course, it ends in the depths of depression. Discouragement weakens us so that we are vulnerable to many other temptations that lurk in the darkness of despondency.

In our imaginations let us journey to the dreary waste of the Arabian desert. We see a man trudging along. His shoulders are bent, and his head hangs. He is the incarnation of exhaustion and despair. This bedraggled man flings himself to the ground and sighs toward the heavens. "I have had enough, Lord," he says. "Take my life; I am no better than my ancestors" (1 Kings 19:4). He lies under a broom tree, this broken and dejected man.

The man is Elijah, one of the greatest prophets of God. A short time before this period of depression, Elijah had battled the prophets of Baal on Mount Carmel and had won an overwhelming victory in the presence of the multitudes. God had answered his prayer, and fire consumed the altar drenched with water. In that episode Elijah was the embodiment of dauntless faith and courage. We even meet this man in the New Testament, as he appeared with Moses when Jesus was transfigured on the mountain (Luke 9:28-36).

What was wrong with this man of God when he wanted to throw in the towel and give up on life? There are three things we must take into consideration. First, Elijah was physically exhausted. He had been on the run for many miles as he endeavored to escape the wrath of King Ahab and Queen Jezebel. Often we, too, are most susceptible to temptation when we are sick or physically and emotionally run down. Remember that Christ was tempted in the wilderness when he had been there 40 days fasting. If the mind or body is weak, Satan will try to take advantage of the situation. John Tyndall, a famous 19th-century Irish physicist, suffered from a depression of his chest. He said he was always careful not to necessarily accept as true the opinions and verdicts that came to him in times of depression and sickness. When did the ancient navigator "shoot the sun"? Of course, the only possible and reliable time is when the sun or stars are visible.

A second reason might be advanced for Elijah's discouragement. He enlarged his adversary. It is true Ahab and Jezebel were out to get him. Elijah magnified that and thought everyone was against him. We all tend to think that way. Someone says something unkind about us, and we think that all others have the same opinion. Satan wants to get us into a state of self-pity.

Thirdly, Elijah thought that since nobody seemed to be with him, he was the only true-blue follower of God. Twice he stated his wrong notion: "I am the only one left, and now they are trying to kill me too" (1 Kings 19:10, 14). God had no time for this ungrounded complaining of self-centered righteousness. He told Elijah, "Yet I reserve seven thousand in Israel—all whose knees have not bowed to Baal and all whose mouths have not kissed him" (1 Kings 19:18).

Three causes of discouragement: physical exhaustion, the feeling that somebody is against us; the conviction that we stand alone. When we permit Satan to magnify those items, we are in trouble. God told Elijah that he had to quit "navel gazing." God told him to get up because there is work to be done. Elijah received the assignment to anoint some leaders. He lost himself in God's work, and the discouragement faded away.

It can still be that way! When discouragement stares you in the face, lift up the shield of faith.

*A bad attitude is a rotten apple that affects all good fruit.*

# 24

# *Ready for Change*

An insurance company used this motto: "Ready for Change." It certainly depicts a good attitude toward facing the tomorrows. When Paul tells us to use the shield of faith, he is presupposing forward movement. There is to be no retreating. There is no equipment mentioned for the protecting of the rear.

God has set us down in a world of uncertainty, with the future hid, where we must take risks to live. Scripture says we live by faith—faith in a good and gracious God. We were made for high adventure. Alfred North Whitehead wrote, "Without adventure civilization is in full decay." This is true also in the individual. God seems to smile on those who step out in total trust.

Hebrews 11 lists the gamblers of faith. By faith Abraham went out, not knowing exactly where he was going. He took a chance with God. By faith Moses chose to identify himself with the uncertain struggles for the Israelites' liberty. So the list goes.

Lin Yutang has traced over four centuries what he calls "the depreciation in the currency of ideals." The 17th century talked of divine purpose, with the Reformation being the highlight. The 18th century talked of reason, and the 19th concentrated on economics. He says the 20th century talks about security, and its slogan could be, "Give me security or give me death!"

This type of thinking can seep into our religious consciousness: "Lord, make us comfortable; keep us safe, may the wages stay high and the collateral sure." We talk more about religion being a refuge than an army on the march. Ralph Pulitzer has said, "Monotony is the awful penalty of the careful." Holding our own cannot be the primary task of the church. Faith is a journey, not a set of fixed, bloodless ideas. It is rather betting your life on God and moving into a changing world with God. There will be no bundle of certainties, paid-up insurance, or insulation from danger.

Faith is active. It is not lying at anchor or merely drifting. It is letting go of the past and moving with a quiet confidence into the future. This problem is described by Charles Schultz's comic-strip characters. Snoopy the dog has a great fondness for the past, particularly for the Daisy Hill Puppy Farm. Periodically he makes a visit to his first home. On one occasion Snoopy returns only to discover that the puppy farm has been replaced by a parking garage. As the cars go in and out Snoopy cries, "I can't stand it! You stupid people! You are parking on my memories!" To be sure, memories are wonderful, but they are only a part of the past journey. We must keep on walking, for life lies ahead.

I have always been intrigued by the life and writing of Henry Thoreau. For a while he left Concord, Massachusetts, and went to the woods, to Walden Pond. There he built a cabin and supported himself through his own toil. There he thought and wrote. After two years he returned to the city life. He described his decision in this way: "I left the woods for as good a reason as I went there. Perhaps it seemed to me that I had several more lives to live, and could not spare any more time for that one." That is a marvelous and adventuresome attitude. It is in keeping with the feeling of Pablo Casals, the world-renowned cellist. On his 93rd birthday he said, "Every day I am reborn, every day is a new lifetime for me."

One of Satan's fiery darts endeavors to block us from blossoming to our full potential and completing the mission of our lives. Fear of change will shortchange us. "Faith is being sure of what we hope for and certain of what we do not see" (Heb. 11:1). That is a good shield. "We intend to die by this faith; why should we not live by it?" said Martin Luther.

*Fear of change will shortchange us.*

# 25

# *Faith Encounters Faith*

One of the great roadside rescues of history was the healing of the blind man Bartimaeus. Jesus and his disciples were being encompassed by a great crowd as they were leaving Jericho. Blind Bartimaeus was sitting along the side of the road. It was business as usual for him, for he was a beggar. He had heard the people buzzing about Jesus and had learned about some mighty things that this man from Nazareth had done. On impulse Bartimaeus thought, "Maybe he can do something for me." So he cried out, "Jesus, Son of David, have mercy on me!"

The crowds didn't like the interruption. They didn't want anyone to crash their party with cries for attention. They were upset, like some people are when a baby cries in church. So the crowd reacted unfavorably to this beseeching beggar who was messing up their meeting with Jesus. Mark simply says that the crowd rebuked the blind man, telling him to be quiet (10:48).

At this point Bartimaeus could have withdrawn into his shell and just accepted his condition as a frustration of fate. Many thoughts could have gone through his mind in frenzied flashes. "I am a poor, insignificant man and have no right to claim the time and attention of

81

Jesus. . . . Maybe he will come by some day alone, and then I will try again. . . . Maybe I should stick to my begging and stop thinking there is something better for me. . . . Maybe if I am supposed to be healed it will happen whether I call on Jesus or not. . . . Maybe fate is the master of my destiny."

Bartimaeus could not accept these flashing thoughts. The crowd was throwing darts of denunciation for his outburst, but Bartimaeus held forth the shield of faith, and the cutting comments of the crowd fell harmlessly to the ground. Scripture says, "he shouted all the more." Faith—not fate—was going to have the final word.

And Jesus stopped. The parade came to a halt, for Jesus appreciated the worth of a single person. Jesus then said to the crowd, "Call him." And the blind man received his sight.

I would like to reach across the centuries and shake the hand of Bartimaeus. He was a man determined not to miss an opportunity. He knew what he really wanted, and when the moment came, he seized it. The crowd did not control his behavior. His faith did not fold under the pressure of the folks who were following Jesus. He was willing to pipe up in the midst of his peers. Emerson paints a telling picture about those who are not willing to make those decisions: "Some men live on the brink of mysteries into which they never enter; and with their hand on the doorlatch, they die outside."

The blind Bartimaeus is an example of one who warded off the negative darts of those who would hold us back from discoveries of faith. We open the door for miracles to happen when there is a spirit of imagination, daring, and courage.

Bartimaeus reminds me of the crocus flower, the pioneer of the early bloomers. It does not wait until the snow gets off the ground. It pushes up through, and its sword-shaped leaves seem to say, "Get out of the way, Winter. Spring is coming, and I want to greet the season." Other flowers may sleep until May or June, but the crocus dares to jump the gun and take a chance.

Blind Bartimaeus was like that. The crowd covered him, but he pushed through the din of conversation with a plea for mercy. It seemed impossible to break through the darkness into light. But with God all things are possible. And that day Bartimaeus broke into full bloom as he was touched by the springtime of Jesus. It would not have happened without the shield of faith which blocked out the cries of the crowd.

*Doubt blocks possibilities; faith pursues possibilities.*

# 26

# Hug a Tree

Some high-school youth were backpacking in the Colorado Rockies. As they were getting their gear and provisions in order, the guide presented them with some precautions. One thing he told them was to "hug a tree." He was not giving a lecture on affection for trees. He knew that often on backpacking trips a youth would wander from the group on an exploratory trip of his or her own. Soon the hiker would be lost in the wooded mountain terrain. The guide told them the best thing to do then was to "hug a tree." The tree wouldn't move, so the lost backpacker would stay put. Help would soon come. If the lost one kept walking, he or she would usually get farther and farther from the rest of the group, thus making the search more difficult.

Life sometimes is like a deep, mysterious woods. It is easy to get lost and to wander aimlessly, with plenty of motion but no direction. We need to stop and get our bearings. We need to "hug a tree." And the one I recommend is the "Root of Jesse" (Isa. 11:10). That mighty tree is Jesus Christ. When you embrace him in faith, the lost is found. Deliverance and salvation have arrived at the scene of your lostness.

Objectively, salvation may mean all the drama of God's saving acts in history, culminating in the crowning work of Calvary. Subjectively, it also means the personal appropriation of those saving acts in experience. Salvation is not agreement with a principle, but a relationship of trust with a person, Jesus Christ. Paul says, "I want to know Christ and the power of his resurrection" (Phil. 3:10).

It is like swimming. No one ever learned to swim by theory alone. A teacher may explain and demonstrate, but the time comes when the pupil has to get into the water and trust himself or herself to its supporting power. This knowledge comes through personal experience. The parent who says that his or her son was never going swimming until he knew how is talking nonsense. Trusting the water is a necessary part of knowing how. Without that trust the knowledge remains merely an academic thing.

A pioneer reached the banks of the mighty Mississippi River early in the winter when ice covered the surface. Because he didn't know how thick the ice was, he hesitated a long time before crossing over. But night was approaching, and he had to reach the other side before dark. Finally, with fear and anxiety, he crept on his hands and knees to distribute his weight more evenly. Every little cracking sound sent shivers up and down his spine. When he had crawled about halfway across the great river, he heard singing and hoofbeats behind him. There in the gathering darkness was a man driving a four-horse-sleigh load of coal across the ice, singing as he went. That man evidently knew that the ice was thick enough to support tons of weight.

Paul tells us to take the "helmet of salvation" (Eph. 6:17). The assurance of salvation is necessary if one is to walk and run confidently in life. When you know that forgiveness is a present reality, you are then set free to serve God and enjoy God forever.

But how does the certainty come? Feeling can be deceiving, and our emotions can play tricks on us. We must go to the Word of God to receive the helmet of salvation which keeps our minds on Christ Jesus. That Word says, "To all who received him, to those who believed in his name, he gave the right to become children of God" (John 1:12).

When God speaks, we must shut up and listen. Take God at his word. That's faith and with it salvation—now and forever!

*The world is slippery, and everyone needs something to hold on to.*

# 27

# A Helmet of Hope

As we look at the armor of God for the Christian soldier, we find one piece of equipment that is still used in modern warfare. It is the helmet. Paul tells the church at Ephesus that the helmet is salvation. In his first letter to the Thessalonians, Paul is more explicit. He says, "the hope of salvation is a helmet" (5:8).

Hope is a present sustaining attitude and also a future promise. Salvation is a present reality and also a future inheritance. Paul gives the following benediction to the church at Rome, "May the God of hope fill you with all joy and peace as you trust in him, so that you may overflow with hope by the power of the Holy Spirit" (Rom. 15:13).

Paul also tells the Christian believers about the raw materials out of which hope is fashioned. "Not only so, but we also rejoice in our sufferings, because we know that suffering produces perseverance; perseverance, character; and character, hope. Hope does not disappoint us, because God has poured out his love into our hearts by the Holy Spirit, whom he has given us (Rom. 5:3-5).

Suffering is something we usually try to avoid. Yet it will always come in some shape sooner or later. It can trip us up, or by God's grace the bumps can be transformed into stepping-stones. Paul tells Timothy, "Endure hardship with us like a good soldier of Christ Jesus" (2 Tim. 2:3). There is an old adage: "The north wind made the Vikings." Struggle can put color in the blood, confidence in the soul, light in the eyes, steel in the backbone. Arnold Toynbee states that "It is difficulties and obstacles that can lead to the flowering of a civilization." Flowers grown in a protective hothouse will not be able to withstand the elements of nature. Neither will humans.

Suffering leads to perseverance, the next rung on the ladder. Perseverance is staying power, and Scripture talks about "enduring to the end." Someone has defined a diamond as a "piece of coal which stayed on the job." People often lose out because they lack staying power. They leave for greener pastures just before the grass starts growing on their own plot.

Perseverance produces character. It is the finished product. The oak tree, bent and twisted by adversity, stands solid with its scars as testimony of its life's story. The King James version of the Bible uses the word "experience" instead of character. Edwin Aubrey translates the verse in this way: "The pressures of life develop staying power, and staying power develops competence, and competence develops hope."

Dr. Ernest Gordon in his book *Through the Valley of the Kwai*, himself a prisoner of war, said that as some of the longtime prisoners marched into camp it was quite evident that they were marked for death. They lacked both faith and hope. As they trudged wearily along, he said, "Their faces were expressionless. The inner spark had been quenched. They had come here to die. Many had no recognizable disease that the doctors could treat in any way. They were waiting for death."

We can endure just about anything if we have hope. Without it we cannot survive. William James, a great psychologist, described a time in his early life when he was in the grip of a deep despair: "Fear was so incisive and powerful that if I had not clung to scripture texts like 'The eternal God is my refuge,' and 'Come unto me all ye that labor and are heavy laden,' and 'I am the resurrection and the life,' I think I should really have gone insane." God has the last word. Nothing can separate us from God's love. You are more than conquerors through God. Wear that hat. It is your helmet of salvation.

*Where there is hope, there is life.*

# 28

# *The Salvation Blanket*

One of man's basic needs, according to psychologist Abraham Maslow, is security. We refer to stocks and bonds as securities, an investment for a secure future. Much talk today revolves around national security. People panic when they hear of the shortcomings of our Social Security system. Homes are protected from robbers by security locks and systems. We are a security-conscious people.

In the comic strip *Peanuts* Linus has a security blanket which is very dear to him. In one episode, Snoopy, the mischievous dog, snatches the blanket and flies out into the winter cold. Linus rushes outside and does battle with Snoopy over the blanket.

When he finally wins and stands at the front door, completely exhausted, his sister, Lucy, admonished him, "Are you crazy? It is cold outside! You could catch pneumonia rolling around out there in the snow."

Linus replies, "The struggle for security knows no season!"

When Paul urges us to wear "the helmet of salvation," we could interpret that as our security blanket. God doesn't come to coddle us, but he does want us to live in confidence and assurance that he will provide for our needs. Paul says, "And my God will meet all your needs according to his glorious riches in Christ Jesus" (Phil. 4:19). Having a security blanket in God, we can endure the loss of other securities when they are wrested from us.

One of our problems seems to be that we think we must earn or struggle to achieve security. The rich seem to have more security because they can afford it. When we carry this thinking into the realm of faith, we get confused. Security, or salvation, comes from God. It is God's gift. Moses sings, "The Lord is my strength and my song, he has become my salvation" (Exod. 15:2). David shouts, "The Lord is my light and my salvation—whom shall I fear?" (Psalm 27:1). And when Zacchaeus has Jesus as a supper guest it ends up with Zacchaeus being a changed man. Jesus says, "Today salvation has come to this house" (Luke 19:9).

This security comes freely from God to the penitent, believing sinner. And God is not whimsical, yanking it away from us as Snoopy did to Linus. Yet many Christians live in insecurity, thinking that salvation slips in and out the doorway. They are constantly running out in the cold trying to catch this illusive blanket. In Shakespeare's *Hamlet* the melancholy Dane plots to kill his uncle, the King of Denmark. It is revenge because his uncle had murdered Hamlet's father. In one scene Hamlet surprises the king at prayer and is about to stab him when he decides this would be a kindness, since the king would then go to heaven. Hamlet resolves to wait until he can catch his uncle in sin; then he will kill the guilty man and send him straight to hell.

This notion haunts many Christians and robs us of our

security. If we should die while in a fit of anger, would we go to hell? If we succumbed of a heart attack while seeing a naughty movie, would we be forever separated from the love of God? The reasoning that accepts those notions is based on a wrong idea about God. We will always be sinners, even though forgiven. God does not pop in and out every time our thoughts change from good to bad or our behavior is noble or ignoble. Sin is taken seriously, but forgiveness is bigger. Salvation from God is a covenant, and God doesn't abandon us when we slip and fall in our Christian walk. God stays right with us to pick us up again.

That salvation is my security blanket. It is my helmet, for it protects my fickle mind and gives it stability. "Therefore, there is now no condemnation for those who are in Christ Jesus" (Rom. 8:1).

*Security comes from putting stock in salvation.*

# 29

# Salvation from Stalemate

A popular television series entitled *Mission Impossible* began with a tape recorder informing the hero of a mission that seemed impossible. Before the tape would self-destruct, it would always end with these words, "This is your mission, should you choose to accept it!" Of course, the hero always did—or there would have been no television show.

The Israelite people were once faced with such a choice. After escaping their Egyptian taskmasters they had a brief sojourn at Mount Sinai. Then they went to Kadesh on the border of Caanan, the Promised Land. Moses, their venerable leader, sent 12 scouts to spy on the fortifications protecting it, so that he might plan a strategy for conquering the land. When the spies returned, they all agreed that the land was productive—a land flowing with milk and honey. But 10 of them exclaimed, "The inhabitants are like giants, and we are like grasshoppers. We cannot conquer this land!" Two of the spies, Joshua and Caleb, granted that the land was well fortified, but they stated, "The Lord is with us and we can take the land; let us move forward."

Israel did not choose to accept their mission. They

accepted the majority report. As a consequence, they wandered for 40 years until God raised up another generation that had faith to move forward and possess the land. Only Joshua and Caleb, the two men of faith of the former generation, entered the Promised Land. The others all died on the east side of the Jordan.

Even though the people had seen the deliverance or salvation of the Lord many times, they were reluctant to think and act accordingly. Thus stalemate set in with its accompanying stagnation. Arnold Toynbee, a historian, points out how people came to the Easter Island from far across the Pacific and somehow made those huge statues that dot the landscape. Then they ventured forth no more. What pathetic and deadly words: "they ventured forth no more." They were unwilling to leave the familiar for the future with faith.

When Paul urges us to wear the "helmet of salvation" I believe he wants us to have confidence in God. Think of a big God, and your thoughts will be accordingly. Think of your problems rather than God's power and you will be reluctant to risk reaching out. The poet Milton was profoundly right when he wrote:

The mind is its own place, and in itself
Can make a heaven of hell, a hell of heaven.

The psalmist was wearing the helmet of salvation (deliverance thinking) when he wrote: "You answer us with awesome deeds of righteousness, O God our savior, the hope of all the ends of the earth and of the farthest seas" (Ps. 65:5).

There is a story of Houdini, the magician, which

might be legendary but profound in meaning. Houdini had a standing challenge that he could get out of any locked jail in 60 minutes, providing he could enter with street clothes and not be observed in his work. A little town in the British Isles decided to challenge him and perhaps embarrass the great Houdini. This town had just completed an escape-proof jail, so they invited Houdini to come and see if he could break out.

He accepted the invitation. He was allowed to enter the jail in street clothes. The cell door clanged shut with the sound of heavy steel. Houdini went to work. He had a long flexible steel rod hid in his belt which he used to try tripping the lock. He worked for 30 minutes, 45 minutes, and then an hour passed and he was perspiring. After two hours he was exhausted. He leaned against the door, and to his amazement it opened. They had never locked the door. It was their trick on the great escape artist. The door was only locked in Houdini's mind.

The helmet of salvation keeps us from having doors locked in our minds!

*Salvation shapes the human soul.*

# 30

# You Have Passed

Remember your college days when the judgment of final exams put you on edge? So much was at stake. However, a few teachers offered an exemption from the rigorous cramming which marked the exam season. Those students whose daily work had been competent and whose term papers were of good quality would be excused from the final test. Perhaps the teacher would put a list on the board a week or two before finals. That list would contain the names of those who could breathe easily, for they had already passed with flying colors. As a student's eyes would run down the list, his heart would be pumping loud and fast. Then his eyes would focus on his name! Eureka! No final examination. No judgment —just life.

It is that way in the Christian life. When Paul tells us to wear the "helmet of salvation" I believe that he encourages us to live in the freedom and exhilaration of knowing that eternal life is a present possession for those who believe in the Christ. Therefore, we don't tremble during talk of impending judgment. We don't worry about standing before the living Lord at the last day.

We have already been accepted to move into the next classroom—God's imperishable palace.

"I tell you the truth, whoever hears my word and believes him who sent me has eternal life and will not be condemned; he has crossed over from death to life" (John 5:24).

Some years ago the movie actress Deborah Kerr was interviewed concerning her experiences making the film *Quo Vadis*. At one point the lions rushed at her when she was tied to a stake in the Roman Colosseum.

The reporter asked her, "Weren't you afraid when the lions made a rush at you?"

She replied, "No, I am one of those actresses who reads all the script of a movie. I had read to the end of the script, and I knew that Robert Taylor would come and rescue me."

That is a good statement to keep in your heart and mind: "I had read the script to the end." Many of us have failed to do that. Not knowing how it ends can send chills up and down the spine. Jesus has overcome the world. Paul lists many things that confront us and then exclaims, "nor anything else in all creation, will be able to separate us from the love of God that is in Christ Jesus our Lord" (Rom. 8:38). That promise protects us from the darts of doubt. It is a good helmet.

Dietrich Bonhoeffer, church leader in Germany at the time of Hitler's rise to power, wore the "helmet of salvation." His opposition to the Nazi regime ended in his imprisonment in 1943. In prison his indomitable courage and Christian inspiration left its mark on both fellow prisoners and guards. His letters and papers smuggled out of prison have blessed later generations.

A British officer who was with him in prison told of a service which Bonhoeffer conducted on Sunday, April 8, 1945. He said that Bonhoeffer spoke just the right words to give his fellow prisoners hope. And before Bonhoeffer finished his last prayer two evil-looking men came in and said, "Prisoner Bonhoeffer, get ready to come with us." Those words meant only one thing—the scaffold. As the prisoners bade him good-bye, Bonhoeffer turned to the British officer and said, "This is the end. For me the beginning of life." The next day he was hanged.

When you wear the helmet of salvation, you are freed from the fear of life and of death. You are in the keeping of the Lord of life. In Christ you have passed. Let's celebrate! Let's sing a song of salvation!

*Salvation smothers judgment jitters.*

# 31

# On the Attack

Paul gives one offensive weapon to the Christian soldier. Into the Christian's hands he places the sword of the Spirit, which is the Word of God. The Christian is called not only to withstand evil, but also to fight for the good. Scripture says, "For the word of God is living and active. Sharper than any double-edged sword, it penetrates even to dividing soul and spirit, joints and marrow; it judges the thoughts and attitudes of the heart" (Heb. 4:12).

A preacher went to serve a congregation in a very rural community. Soon after arriving, he called a meeting of the church officials. They seemed determined to assist him by telling him certain subjects that should not be expounded from the pulpit. "Don't say anything against liquor," one suggested, "because one of our largest contributors owns the biggest still in these parts. Don't talk about gambling, because some of your prominent members have a little poker game each week."

"I would advise," said another, "that you go easy on the subject of gossip, because this is a prevailing pastime in this town."

The startled preacher asked, "What on earth can I preach?"

"I know," exclaimed one member. "Talk about the Jews. There isn't one in a hundred miles of this place."

People so often go with the flow. They don't want to stand in opposition to anything—even the wrong thing. Billy Sunday, the fiery evangelist of a previous generation, was often accused of creating turmoil everywhere he went. "The trouble with you, Billy," said a friend, "is that you are always rubbing the dog's fur the wrong way."

In reply Billy made a whimsical and masterful observation: "It is also possible that the dog is turned the wrong way."

To be sure, the good news of Jesus Christ is the main diet of proclamation from the pulpit and from the platform of your vocation. But wrong must be denounced also. Evil must be unmasked. Henri Frederic Amiel, a Swiss author, said, "Truth is violated by falsehood, but is outraged by silence." If we sit quietly on the sidelines while evil marches on the field, we abdicate our Christian calling. Shakespeare observed in *King Henry VI*, "A little fire is quickly trodden out; which, being suffered, rivers cannot quench."

We must remember that although Jesus admonished the scribes and the Pharisees not to stone the adulteress unless they themselves were without sin, still he commanded the woman to sin no more. To be charitable about the weakness of another person does not require silence about misdeeds. Unless good speaks out, society is like a small child who keeps going a little farther to see how much he can get away with.

Moral neutrality cannot be supported. The sword of the Spirit must be wielded in the attack of evil dragons that still roam the streets of the 20th century. Billy Graham said, "Silence may be golden, but sometimes it is just plain yellow."

A 19th-century prince of the pulpit was Phillips Brooks. He told some fellow precahers: "If you are afraid of men and a slave to their opinions, go and do something else. Go and make shoes to fit them. Go even and paint pictures which you know are bad but which will suit their bad taste. But do not keep on all your life preaching sermons which shall say not what God sent you to declare, but what they hire you to say."

As the children of God we should all take that sword which is God's Word and use it. Sometimes we will afflict the comfortable and sometimes comfort the afflicted. Perhaps a sad epitaph for any of us would be, "He (or she) never offended anyone." The sword is sharp, and the words then should not be blunt!

*Rivers are crooked because they flow in the path of least resistance.*

# 32

# The Cutting Edge

When a movie producer is not satisfied with the way a scene is shaping up, the producer will call for the cameraman to "cut." The acting stops, corrections are made, and then the camera will start rolling again. You cannot continue with a bad performance. This decision to "cut" is essential also in the drama of everyday life. A person must learn how to say no. The sword of the Spirit must slice into life when the tumor of evil is taking hold.

I received an anonymous letter which illustrates this drama. One paragraph read: "I have been seeing a man now for the past year and a half. I love him in many ways that I didn't even know existed in my relationship before. It was like a dream, an answer to my prayers. He needs me, and what a great feeling that is, to need and to be needed. But he is married. Why did God hurt me again? Why was I attracted to him and he to me? I'm not sure I'll be able to cope with this pressure. He has two children, six and eight. . . ."

What was the crux of her problem? Was it not that she continued in a relationship that she should have known was wrong from the very start? She should have hollered, "Cut" before she got so involved in a losing dilemma. God was not hurting her. She was hurting herself.

Joseph of Old Testament times serves us well as a positive example. Potiphar's wife had designs on this young, virile man. She tried all her seductive charm to bed him down. But Joseph refused. Joseph could have made a great case for accepting her invitation. He didn't initiate it. Any red-blooded Hebrew boy would have felt flattered. After all, the playboy philosophy is to enjoy any pleasure served up on the platter of life. But Joseph said no. He turned his back and fled. In doing so he said, "How then can I do such a wicked thing and sin against God?" (Gen. 39:9). He paid a price for this rejection when Potiphar's wife brought false charges against him. He was truly persecuted "for righteousness' sake."

But is not this the nature of the Christian life? It involves the courage to choose the costliness of ultimate loyalties over the cheapness of partial commitments. It is holding on to the abiding joys, rather than the way of quick kicks and quick profits.

In a logging area a long chute extended down the slope of the valley to the river below. The chute was made for logs, but it also served as a good slide for the lumbermen when they wanted to save time going down the treacherous hillside. As one of the lumbermen was tobogganing down the chute, his foot got caught in a hole. As he was trying to free himself, he heard the rumble of logs on the chute above him and knew the impact would kill him. There was only one thing to do. He grabbed his axe and with a mighty swing cut off his foot. He jumped clear of the cascading logs in the nick of time.

He would be crippled for life, but at least he was alive.

Life is sometimes that way. The decision to cut is costly, but necessary for the ultimate good. Jesus said it this way; "If your right eye causes you to sin, gouge it out and throw it away. It is better for you to lose one part of your body than for your whole body to be thrown into hell. And if your right hand causes you to sin, cut it off and throw it away. It is better for you to lose one part of your body than for your whole body to go into hell" (Matt. 5:29-30).

The Word of God is our sword and provides the cutting edge. It is needed to prune for more productivity. When wielded properly it cuts out the cancer of evil. The art of cutting is crucial to a Christian's good health.

*A pruned life is a more productive life.*

# 33

# The Sword and the Swath

The machete is a broad-bladed knife two to three feet in length. It is used especially in South America and in the West Indies for cutting cane and for clearing paths. Jungle fighters often have used machetes in moving through dense underbrush. Life sometimes gets very tangled and we seem to be caught in the underbrush of anxieties and fears. How do we hack our way out? In a sense the "sword of the Spirit, which is the word of God" becomes the machete for the Christian.

The theologian Paul Tillich traced the anxiety of our age to three main sources: the presence of guilt, the fear of meaninglessness, and the inevitability of death. The "sword of the Spirit" can surely slice through these barriers that block the strides of the soul.

I heard about a man who was being tried in court. After the case was completed, the jury withdrew to contemplate the verdict. The man being tried had another engagement so he rushed to the airport to catch a plane for a distant city. He requested his lawyer to send him a telegram when the jury reached their verdict. When he was registered at the hotel in the city of his destination, the hotel clerk handed him a telegram. He knew it was from his lawyer. He anxiously opened it and saw just two words: "Justice prevailed."

Quickly he went to the telephone and sent a telegram to his lawyer, saying, "Appeal immediately." The lawyer's telegram meant he was aquitted. But the man felt guilty—perhaps because he was guilty.

One of our greatest fears is that we will get what we deserve. The cloud of guilt prevents the sun from shining on multitudes. Only a word from God can set us free from our yesterdays. "If we confess our sins, he is faithful and just and will forgive us our sins and purify us from all unrighteousness" (1 John 1:9). The next time Satan tries to take you on a guilt trip, stop him with the sword of the Spirit.

Secondly, we need to clear a path through the jungle of meaninglessness. At times we may have experienced the words of Edna St. Vincent Millay, "Life must go on—I forget just why." History often seems to be a dead-end street. This terrestial ball on which we live has developed into a potential firecracker. Population figures give us claustrophobia. Some ecologists tell us that the rain drops now falling on our heads contain acid.

A novel by George Moore tells of some Irishmen who were given work during the Great Depression. The task was building a road that led into a swamp. Its only purpose was to provide employment. After a few days the men threw down the tools and refused to go on because "for men to work and live they must have an end in view. The road to nowhere cannot be made even though starving men are employed at it."

Joy will be great when a person lives with a purpose. It must be well-defined and worth his while. God gives just that. He asks us to team up with him and work in and for a kingdom that will never end. Paul must have felt this exhilaration when he wrote, "We are therefore Christ's ambassadors" (2 Cor. 5:20). Try on that calling, and meaninglessness will evaporate.

Thirdly, we need to overcome the darkness of death. In most situations we can regroup, correct, try again. But death confronts us with the irretrievable; the account is closed. What then? The only equipment we have to fight with is the "sword of the Spirit which is the word of God." That word is one of hope and promise, based on the resurrection of Jesus. God cut a swath through death, so we will be able to walk through to God's place of high adventure. Paul says, "We will all be changed—in a flash, in the twinkling of an eye" (1 Cor. 15:51-52). The sword of the Spirit cuts through the jungles of fear, and we are set free to walk tall under the banner of Christ.

*Don't run around when you can walk through!*

# 34

# The Power of the Word

"In the beginning was the Word, and the Word was with God and the Word was God. . . . The Word became flesh . . ." (John 1:14). There is power in the Word. Martin Luther stressed this in the great hymn, "A Mighty Fortress," when he wrote, "One little word subdues him" (© 1978 *LBW*). Satan can be held at bay by a word. Paul tells us that the Christian goes to war with the "sword of the Spirit, which is the Word of God" (Eph. 6:17).

Words are really condensed history. They tell stories and transmit meanings. A word can excite you, or a word can depress you. Words can make you sad or glad or mad. "The pen is mightier than the sword," wrote Bulwer Lytton. Jack London, the great writer of wilderness stories, said, "The printer's ink is more intoxicating than whiskey."

When Christ was tempted in the wilderness he answered Satan with the Word. "It is written," he declared. He fought off Satan's savage attacks with the Word.

In a world where the battles of good and evil are gaining in intensity we must learn to use the sword of words.

We cannot afford to be inept in our handling of the Word with our words.

A postal carrier paused at the door of a house to chat with a little girl about her baby brother. The carrier asked her whether her baby brother could talk. She answered, "No. He has his teeth, but his words haven't come in yet." The problem often remains into adulthood. The right words aren't being spoken.

If we are to wield the sword of the Spirit with effectiveness, our words must have three characteristics. They must be clear. They must have color. They must have consistency.

In a sophisticated era we often think that thoughts of obscurity and mysterious depth are signs of a genius. Profundity does not have to be unintelligible to the common person. Communication must be gauged by whether the meaning is clear. Because of our poverty of the right words we often send mixed messages that are confusing. When Ronald Reagan was pushing for a larger military budget, an editorial said that Reagan wanted to "send a message to the Soviet Union." But what kind of message? Fear? War? Intimidation? Our words and our actions always send messages, but the meanings are not often clear. They are as ambiguous as some modern abstract paintings, whose meaning is determined by the eye of the beholder. The church cannot afford this luxury of puzzlement.

Second, our words must have color. Advertisers have learned the art of making words dance. The words are colorful and stir the feelings and set the imagination on fire. Sporting events on television, especially football, have "color commentators." These people do not do the main broadcasting, but throw in comments that add life to the watching of the game.

Think back to your high-school English class. You may have forgotten most of Shakespeare but you will not forget Lady Macbeth washing her hands, crying, "Out, damned spot!" The blood on that woman's hands sticks in the mind.

Or when England was reeling under Nazi fire, Winston Churchill could have said, "Well, folks, let us be strong and keep our courage." Instead, his words had color; they were vibrant: "I have nothing to offer but blood, toil, tears and sweat." Words like that lifted a groggy nation to its feet.

Third, the words we use must have consistency. They must be lived out. Jesus was the Word. That Word "became flesh and lived for a while among us" (John 1:14). Freedom, love, justice, mercy—all came to life in Jesus. The story of redemption was spelled out in him. The Word was wrapped up in a person, and it was delivered first class. Our words, patterned after his Word, will be effective in fighting evil when they are clear, colorful, and consistent.

*Wrestling with words is a noble task.*

# 35

# A Law of Expression

An old captain of a fishing vessel was asked what he did when a storm caught him on the high seas. He replied, "I turn my boat directly into the storm and open up the throttle to full speed ahead. I know if I veer just a bit to either port or starboard, we would be capsized. Our only chance is to face into the storm and give the engine full speed ahead."

This seemed to be Jesus' approach to ministry: to achieve, one must learn to face the winds of opposition and give full strength to going forward. Jesus did not run when obstacles loomed before him.

When he preached in Nazareth, his hometown, he said some things that rattled the folks. They promptly took him to the hill outside town to throw him off. "But he walked right through the crowd and went on his way" (Luke 4:30). Right through the opposition he went, and not a person laid a hand on him.

Later came the time for him to prepare himself for the trip that would end in Jerusalem. The disciples warned him that this would be a fool's errand. Jesus showed his resolve by setting his face to go to Jerusalem, straight into the storm.

Recall, too, the week of the crucifixion. Jesus could have escaped, but he carried out his mission—all the way to the cross.

The Christian must face life with "hats off to the past —coats off to the future." When Paul tells us to take the sword of the Spirit, he implies that we are to be on the offensive. We are to take the Word into the streets, the halls of Congress, and the far-flung beaches of the Pacific.

We have been told that the church that doesn't reach out will pass out. We are, however, usually slow to act on that truth. Jesus said, "You will receive power when the Holy Spirit comes on you; and you will be my witnesses in Jerusalem, and in all Judea and Samaria, and to the end of the earth" (Acts 1:8). Power and confidence come to the soldier who advances and achieves a taste of victory. Note that Jesus links the power of the Spirit with witnessing to Christ. The church lacking power will be the church that sits comfortably without reaching out in witness.

Someone has stated that "Impression without expression leads to depression." If the good news of Jesus touches my soul and warms my heart, there needs to be an outlet for this river of life and freshness. If not, stagnation will set in as surely as in a swamp which receives but does not give.

There is a law governing all friendships: the more frequently you give expression to the feelings within you, the more real those feelings will become. During my first year as a pastor I was a bachelor. I had met a young, beautiful brunette who was going to be teaching in California the following school year. Before she

112

left, she gave me her friendship ring to wear. It was so small it almost cut off the circulation in my little finger. I wore it anyway, even though my finger almost turned blue. I wore it so the young people would ask me whose ring it was. It gave me an opportunity to tell them about the woman who would later become my wife. I needed to express my love toward her. It made the love more real, especially since she was many miles away.

We also have a need to witness our love toward Christ in both word and deed. We are exhorted by Scripture to take that word of witness aggressively into both the storms and the still scenes of our existence.

*More power to you is always more power through you.*

# 36

# Are You There, Jesus?

A mother was busy cooking supper in the kitchen and asked her five-year-old son to go into the pantry to get her a can of tomato soup. The little boy was afraid of the dark and didn't want to go into the old-fashioned pantry alone. He pleaded his case, "Mommy, I'm scared."

Mother responded, "Johnny, be a big, brave boy and just walk in and get it. I need it right away for this food I'm preparing."

Johnny repeated his fear, "Mommy, I'm too scared to go in there by myself."

Mother used a different approach: "It's okay, son. Jesus will be in there with you. Now you go and get mother the soup."

Johnny went to the door and opened it slowly. When he peeked inside it was dark, and he was scared. His hands trembled, but an idea popped into his little head. He said, "Jesus, if you are in there, would you hand me that can of tomato soup?"

At times it is difficult to believe that God is "in there." When illness, death, or tragedy strike us, it may seem that God has vacated the premises. We are so bound to the physical world of flesh and blood that God seems remote. We struggle with communication problems with people around us, so that the folks who are close seem far away. It is not strange then that we have difficulties "seeing" God, who is unseen.

But the promises are there: "Have I not commanded you? Be strong and courageous; do not be terrified; do not be discouraged, for the Lord your God will be with you wherever you go" (Josh. 1:9). "Surely I will be with you always, to the very end of the age" (Matt. 28:20). Henry Ward Beecher, a colonial preacher, claimed these promises. He said, "Time went on, and next came the disclosure of a Christ ever present with me—a Christ that was never far from me, but always near me as a Companion and Friend, to uphold and sustain me. This was the last and best revelation of God's spirit to my soul."

That sounds good, but how does it happen? Paul tells us to "Pray in the Spirit on all occasions" (Eph. 6:18). And again, "Pray continually" (1 Thess. 5:17). Prayer is a channel through which God funnels an awareness of his presence and power. After his Lakers basketball team had won the N.B.A. Championship in 1980, Coach Paul Westhead said of his star player, Magic Johnson, "He realizes the need we have and flows to that need." So does God!

So as we battle discouragement and seem to be all alone and feeling blue, let's dial God and start talking, thinking, and thanking. We might be surprised as we sense what David Livingstone said, "I felt the down-reach of the divine."

I've always been fascinated by explorers who pushed back the boundaries of territories and knowledge. Admiral Richard Byrd did this in the polar regions. At one point he almost reached the place of desperation. He felt that life was nearing its end. His physical strength was gone. Later in his book, *Alone,* he wrote these words: "I solved it by changing my thoughts. When negative thoughts began to come in my mind, I repulsed them and instead filled my mind with thoughts of the presence of God. Suddenly, I had a feeling of confidence and quietness within. The outer situation was just the same, was just as desperate, but it didn't look as difficult, for something had happened inside my mind."

Prayer sends aloft the antenna which receives the signals of him who is called "Immanuel," which means "God with us" (Matt. 1:23).

Don't walk in front of me—
I may not follow:
Don't walk behind me—
I may not lead.
Walk beside me—
And just be my friend.

*Anonymous*

Jesus said, "I have called you friends, for everything that I learned from my Father I have made known to you" (John 15:15).

*A change in outlook may bring outward change.*

# 37

# *Walking in Company*

Paul urged Christians to pray at all times: "Be alert and keep on praying for all the saints. Pray also for me . . ." (Eph. 6:18-19). Prayer can so easily slip into the small world of private needs and personal goals. Rather than including the world when we pray we close out the world. The early church was marked with togetherness in prayers, praise, and possessions (Acts 2:42-47). That intercessory concern for others must again come to the fore in the life of faith.

Florence Allshorn inspired a missionary renewal center in England. She saw a need for a community of healing and restoration for missionaries after a tour of duty. She said, "In the past the emphasis for those trying to live a more dedicated Christian life had been on the need for an unusual effort to alter situations single-handed. Now the leading of the Spirit seemed to be that the witness of living together a truly Christian life was more needed than solitary greatness."

Togetherness rather than solitary greatness is a key concept in the Christian life.

"Doing your own thing" is a slogan of our times. But the solo adventure must give way to the advance of the whole team. The witness of togetherness has greater impact than the single torch of faith standing alone. Life is interdependent. It is a total orchestration. The Christian community demonstrates this through fellowship and praying with and for one another.

We can't make the climb alone. We are indebted to those who gave us our heritage in the gospel. We are dependent on those who travel with us and sustain us. We are helpless and hopeless without the Lord who has gone before us and beckons us onward into the far stretches of eternity.

Intercessory prayer breaks down barriers and establishes open lines of communication between believers. Prayer pulls love out of the basement into the living room. Prayer mobilizes thoughts that are constructive and upbuilding. A team spirit is being molded as hands are uplifted to the Lord of the church. A single snowflake, intricate in design, melts on an extended tongue or is blown away by a soft breath. But if you get enough fragile flakes together, you may have a snowdrift that can stop a train.

Many times the Christian effort in fighting wrong has been dissipated because we have been too proud, stubborn, or unconcerned to band together and present a united front. The purpose of a ship is to sail across the seas—but not all parts of the ship will float. If you take out the engine and put it into the water, it will immediately sink. The propeller, the compass, and many other parts individually would take a rapid trip to the bottom of the sea. But when all the parts of the ship are securely built together, it does sail and it reaches the port of destination.

The Christian life is not supposed to be a lonely picket, but always walking in company. The preacher in the pulpit, the people in the pew, and the shut-in on the shelf all need to be knit together by the thread of intercessory prayer. When Mount Everest was conquered, many applauded the efforts of one or two men. Little did they realize that there were 300 porters in the team that conquered Everest. In *The Conquest of Everest* Hugh Rutledge wrote: "Above all else I should like to stress our unity as a party. This was undoubtedly the biggest single fact in the final result, for the ascent of Everest demanded a high degree of selfless co-operation . . . the story of Everest is one of teamwork."

May that be said of the church of Jesus Christ!

*The Christian life is not a lonely picket.*

# 38

# The Pause That Refreshes

Beautiful Lake Louise is nestled in the snow-covered peaks of the Canadian Rockies. It sparkles like a gem in this setting of splendor. A station wagon loaded with an American tourist family roared into the parking lot by the lake. A woman jumped out of the car with a map in hand and asked a man standing nearby, "Sir, can you tell me where we can find Lake Louise?"

The man, somewhat puzzled, looked strangely at her and said, "But lady, this is Lake Louise!"

The woman then spun around, marked her map, jumped into the wagon, and banged the door closed. She turned to her husband and said, "Well, honey, we've done Lake Louise!" And the car ground off down the highway in a cloud of dust.

Another example of this rushing pace of life is told by Erma Bombeck. She had clipped a newspaper article that said that the average visitor to the Grand Canyon spends an average of four hours there, but only 20 minutes actually looking at the phenomenal gorge. She asked her husband, "Where do you think the tourists spend the rest of their time?"

He replied, "Waiting in line to go to the restrooms."

She responded, "Wrong! They spend their time buying gifts to take home."

We have all been living in a revolving door so much that we forget the art of stopping and standing still. We miss the beauty of a sunset or a field of sunflowers. Our failure to pause and stand, wrapped in awe and wonder, is causing something to die within us. If we cannot bear being alone at times, we show signs of some inner instability.

William Wordsworth said, "How gracious, how benign, is Solitude." After Paul had dressed Christians in combat attire he urged them to pray at all times. Soldiers need furloughs, rest, and relaxation. For Christians, prayer should be the pause that refreshes!

There are many reasons for being alone in communion with God and with the inner you. Sometimes we are paralyzed by the pressures of life and need to unwind and get our bearings again. Grief over the loss of a loved one or the loss of a job may disorient us. Certainly we need the encouragement and comfort of friends, but we also need to sort stuff out alone.

It seems to be a law of nature. I've had animals around me ever since I was a small child. I've noticed that when hurt or injured an animal will crawl into the bushes to lick its wounds. It will even die there alone.

People also react this way. Even Jesus experienced it. When word reached Jesus that his cousin, John the Baptist, had been beheaded by Herod, he wanted to leave everyone. It was not easy, because the crowds were always following him. But Jesus sent away even his disciples so that he could be by himself in communion with his Father. One needs friends near but sometimes not too near.

One needs to be alone usually in creative moments. A great idea is often given birth when a person is alone and not surrounded by the noise of a commotion-filled committee room.

Also in the moment of decision making we need the silence of solitude. Jesus spent time in the wilderness, alone, before he commenced his public ministry. Decisions had to be made concerning the style of his redemptive activity. Before Calvary he was alone in the Garden of Gethsemane. Perhaps everything that was human in him cried out against such an untimely death. Yet after praying he chose the cross. The Father's will prevailed.

Our prayer, too, is not so much an effort to alter the will of God as to discover it. As Christian soldiers, we need to pause in prayer to get our orders straight.

*Prayer is not domineering God's will, but discovering it.*

# 39

# Playing When Hurt

I have always enjoyed watching football on television. Often a player is sent reeling from a hefty blow, or is lying on the field grimacing in pain after a vicious tackle. Slowly the player gets to his feet, shakes his head, and goes back to the huddle for the next play. Then the announcer, with commendation in his voice, says, "That's what I like about that young man: he plays when he's hurt."

It probably is easier to play when hurt when hundreds of thousands of people are watching. It is a dramatic situation, and the adrenalin flows freely. However, when you are alone and dealing with brokenness —whether in relationships or in health—it is much more difficult to play when hurt. The temptation is far greater to crawl into a hole and sweat and sulk. We don't want to muster up our strength to keep playing.

When the apostle Paul wrote the book of Ephesians, he was in prison in Rome. He was somewhat isolated by house arrest, and many of his dreams of being involved in the expansion movement of the Christian faith were put on the shelf. His true character was demonstrated in his prayer requests during imprisonment. "Pray in the Spirit on all occasions with all kinds of prayers and requests. With this in mind, be alert and always keep on praying for all the saints. Pray also for me, that whenever I open my mouth, words may be given to me so that I will fearlessly make known the mystery of the gospel, for which I am an ambassador in chains. Pray that I may declare it fearlessly, as I should" (Eph. 6:18-20). It is interesting that even in imprisonment the apostle Paul did not quit "playing the game." Twice he mentioned that the people of Ephesus should pray that he may speak the gospel in boldness. He did not ask for immunity from his mission.

This same attitude was exhibited by Peter and John. When they had been arrested and then released, they joined Christian friends in a prayer meeting. This is what they requested: "Now, Lord, consider their threats and enable your servants to speak your word with great boldness" (Acts 4:29). You would think that they would have asked God to make the officials go a little easier on them. Perhaps they should have prayed for a little less "contact" in the contest for the souls of people. But no, the early church was willing to play when hurt!

A Christian leader prayed: "Lord, we do not ask for easier lives, but rather to be stronger men. We do not ask for tasks equal to our strength, but for strength equal to any task that comes our way." That is a prayer of courage.

In 1802 Beethoven drew up a will that is a sad document. He felt cheated and hopeless since he had become deaf. The document ended with a burst of feeling, "O Providence, grant me at last but one day of pure joy;

it is so long since real joy echoes in my heart." Twenty-four years later Beethoven was standing in a theater in Vienna. A vast audience had risen to applaud him, shouting their delight at the first performance of the Ninth Symphony, at the end of which the chorus joins with the orchestra, singing the composer's version of Schiller's "Ode to Joy." It had been created in the chambers of deafness, and Beethoven was not able to hear the applause of the audience and he had turned the leaves of his score in silence. But he kept "playing when hurt," and the world has richly been blessed. Prayer can cause something to happen within us that makes all the difference.

*Prayer is more than covering our bets.*

# 40

# Getting in the Groove

Thomas Carlyle said, "Prayer is and remains the native and deepest impulse of the soul of man." Prayer is the umbilical cord through which the life-giving grace of God flows. Disconnected from the life system, our spiritual lives will be snuffed out.

Paul's exhortations to prayer focus on discovering God's will. Prayer is not for the purpose of making God's will conform to our will. That is dangerous business, and it can backfire. We cannot use God! Jesus taught us to pray, "Thy will be done."

I shudder when people think of prayer as a means of letting God know how things should be run. A scientist does not devise an invention or a formula and then demand nature to give him what it takes to make it work. Rather he goes to the laboratory with a humble and inquisitive spirit to learn what things are possible through nature. In science nature's will and secrets come first. In prayer God's will must come first.

When God's will is revealed, we can cooperate with it. Such prayers may not make one wealthy, but they will make one wise. They may not help one beat an enemy, but they will help win a friend. They may not show one how to lighten burdens, but they will show how to bear them.

This understanding of prayer as a search for God's will does not mean that we should cease making our sincere wishes known to God. But it does mean that we must be willing to accept the answer no, without bitterness or loss of faith. We must understand that this would be a chaotic world if Christians could pick answers out of God's storehouse of provision like a person grabbing chocolates out of the candy box. Pious people would be fighting one another with words of prayer, as viciously as they might fight with bullets. Some praying gardener might be requesting God for rain on a Saturday afternoon for his dry soil while a mother is sending an S.O.S. to heaven so it will not rain on her daughter's wedding. People would be afraid of investing in the stock market lest some saintly soul desiring to sell short were to pray all night for the market to take a turn down after some other saint prayed only half the night for it to go up.

Therefore Scripture exhorts us to pray "in the Spirit" and to make our requests "in Jesus' name." This means to ask in accordance with his will. We are in effect saying, "This is what Christ wants." There are no magical formulas here for manipulating God. Oliver Wendell Holmes once said that the power of the Gulf Stream would flow through an ordinary drinking straw if it were placed parallel with the direction of the stream. If not, the straw would be bounced to and fro. Our lives are like that. Prayer's main function is to line us up with God's purposes and plans. When that happens,

God works through us as channels of his grace and power.

When I was a child, I often saw the motto "Prayer changes things." I believe it to a degree. But I believe even more that "Prayer changes people." Prayer can change me, and then God can use me to change things! God is the boss and not a bellhop. It is God who calls the shots. Thus in prayer, we need to do a lot of listening!

*The potter shapes the clay; the clay's job is to be willing.*